Charles de Gaulle's famous press conference on November 28, 1967, provoked serious alarm in France as well as within Jewish communities throughout the world. Many of the General's comments on Israel— including his characterization of Jews as "an elite people, self-assured and domineering"—drew comparisons with the Protocols of the Elders of Zion and other virulent expressions of European anti-Semitism.

Written before de Gaulle's rejection by the French electorate on April 27, 1969, Raymond Aron's book forms part of the record of Gaullism's final phase. Dr. Aron, one of France's most respected political thinkers and an unflinching critic of the French establishment, provides a dispassionate yet searching analysis of the full record of Gaullist diplomacy in the Middle East during the past two decades. His discussion encompasses the current attitudes of Eastern and Western Europe toward Israel and Zionism, the feelings of non-Israeli Jews—orthodox and assimilated —about Israel, and the intricacies of four-power involvement in the Middle East. Dr. Aron attacks Gaullist policies in the context of these larger issues and traces the roots of de Gaulle's anti-Zionist posture to the Suez Crisis of 1956, when the Israelis, who entered the war independently of France, were judged guilty of *lèse-gaullisme*.

Dr. Aron describes his book as written by "a 'dejudaized' Jew examining his conscience". His concluding essays on the dilemma of European Jews and their position vis-à-vis Israel soberly reflects on the pervasiveness and resilience of European anti-Semitism, whether religious, political or categorical.

The author: Raymond Aron, until recently professor of sociology at the Sorbonne, is a regular contributor to *Encounter*, and to *Le Figaro*, in which many of these essays first appeared.

De Gaulle, Israel and
the Jews

By the same author

Introduction to the Philosophy of History
Eighteen lectures on Industrial Society
Main Currents in Sociological Thought

De Gaulle, Israel and the Jews

Raymond Aron

Translated from the French by John Sturrock

FREDERICK A. PRAEGER, *Publishers*

New York · Washington

BOOKS THAT MATTER
Published in the United States of America in 1969
by Frederick A. Praeger, Inc., Publishers
111 Fourth Avenue, New York, N.Y. 10003

© 1968, in France, by Librairie Plon
English translation © 1969, in London, England
by André Deutsch Ltd.

Library of Congress Catalog Card Number: 69-16702

Printed in Great Britain

Contents

Author's Note

Before this book appeared in English, General de Gaulle had relinquished power, after his rejection by the electorate on April 27, 1969. My dialogue with him has therefore lost all political significance; it belongs to Gaullism's final phase, a few months prior to the crisis of May 1968, which was itself responsible for the referendum and the President's resignation. From now on the book, which is in effect a 'de-judaized' Jew examining his conscience, can be offered free from these other considerations. Its British and American readers can ignore the references to the man who dominated the French and European scene for eleven years and whom I have always respected and very often admired. It is for them to decide whether these texts, which were written on different occasions, have preserved a significance and interest beyond the circumstances that gave rise to them.

Preface

I hesitated a long time before writing 'The Age of Suspicion' and longer still before I published these articles as a book.

If certain voices had made themselves heard, if a Gaullist, François Mauriac or André Malraux, had made the same answer to General de Gaulle at the end of November 1967 that he would have made to any other statesman coming out with such remarks, then I would have stayed out of a debate in which I cannot involve myself altogether calmly. But alas, none of the writers that are a credit to French literature, none of those who so often act as spokesmen for the conscience of mankind, has spoken. And so I resolved or resigned myself not to fill a role to which I cannot aspire but to plead against an indictment that is all the more insidious for having remained camouflaged. The defendant who cannot find an advocate ensures his own defence.

I am not indifferent to certain objections that have been expressed, even by those closest to me. Best to remain silent, they say, on so vexed and inflammatory a subject. You will make the trouble worse by reminding people of it, and furnish arguments to those you are denouncing; you won't ever strike the right note, you will either be too aggressive or too defensive, you will annoy both your non-Jewish fellow-countrymen and your 'co-religionists'. Some of these will think you too detached from Israel, others not detached enough. The radical distinction between Church and State is self-evident to some, others reject it. You are calling on the Jews to tolerate one another and on the French to respect a peculiar situation, that of the Jews who take upon themselves the contradictions of their condition not so much by listening to reason, which they yet regard as the highest value, as by following their emotions; you run the risk of infuriating the lot of them, because everyone wants a solution and you are only offering problems.

Perhaps, as some have said, this little book will do more harm than good. But for all that I shall put my trust in the optimists and hope that my readers, Jews and non-Jews alike, will read the testimony that one man has to give in the spirit in which it was written: not without passion but without bad faith, and with a willingness to understand a destiny that I refuse to shirk.

It occurred to me that the full significance of my testimony would be lost if I did not add to my comments on the Press Conference of 27 November, 1967, the series of articles which I published in the *Figaro* and the *Figaro Littéraire* during May and June 1967, and two other texts, of 1960 and 1962, written in less emotional circumstances. The latter aroused or outraged many French Jews and almost all the Israelis. I reproduce it here simply in order to be fair, so that no one should accuse me of inconsistency, of opportunism or of repudiating my own opinions. In the light of what happened in 1967 many of my 'co-religionists' will perhaps judge this article less harshly now than they did in 1962.

Preface to the English Edition

So that English and American readers will be able to follow the chapter entitled 'The Age of Suspicion', I have thought it necessary to quote here the chief points from General de Gaulle's press conference, held on November 27, 1967:

The setting-up between the two world wars, for we must indeed go back as far as that, of a home for Zionists in Palestine, and the setting-up after the second world war of a State of Israel, both aroused a certain amount of apprehension at the time. One might have asked oneself, and even many Jews asked themselves, whether the planting of this community in lands acquired under more or less justifiable conditions and in the midst of Arab populations fundamentally hostile to it, would not lead to ceaseless and interminable friction and conflict. Some even feared that the Jews, scattered hitherto but who had remained what they had always been, that is an élite people, self-assured and domineering, might, once they were reunited, turn the very moving hopes they had formed over nineteen centuries: 'Next year in Jerusalem', into a burning ambition of conquest. In spite of the wave of ill-feeling, now rising, now falling, which they had provoked, or rather aroused, in certain countries and at certain times, a considerable capital of interest and even sympathy had accrued in their favour, especially, it must be said, in Christendom. A capital born of the immense memory of the Testament, fed by all the sources of a magnificent liturgy, maintained by the pity felt for their ancient misfortunes which, among us, had been turned into poetry by the legend of the 'Wandering Jew', swelled by the abominable persecutions they suffered during the second world war, and magnified since they recovered their homeland by their constructive labours and the courage of their soldiers. That is why, independently of the tremendous

1*

assistance in money, influence and propaganda which the Israelis received from Jewish circles in America and Europe, many countries, and France among them, looked with satisfaction on the setting-up of their State on land granted them by the Powers, while at the same time wanting them to reach a peaceful *modus vivendi* with their neighbours through the use of a little modesty.

It must be said that these basic psychological facts changed somewhat after 1956, thanks to the Franco-British expedition to Suez. Indeed, we watched the emergence of a State of Israel that was warlike and set on expansion. And then the action she was taking to double her population through immigration gave us to think that the territory she had acquired would not suffice her for long and that she would be led to expand it whenever an opportunity arose. This, anyway, was why the Fifth Republic broke away from the special and very close ties which the previous regime had established with Israel. The Fifth Republic was diligent, on the contrary, in seeking a détente in the Middle East. Naturally, we maintained cordial relations with the Israeli government and even provided it, for its defensive needs, with the armaments it had asked to buy. But, at the same time, we freely counselled moderation on them, especially in connection with their legal dispute over the waters of the Jordan, and over the periodic skirmishing which brought the two sides face to face. Finally, we would not endorse that government's move to a part of Jerusalem which it had seized, and we kept our Embassy in Tel Aviv.

On the other hand, once the Algerian affair had been brought to an end, we resumed the same policy of friendship and co-operation with the Arab peoples of the East which had been France's policy in that part of the world for centuries past; this policy, with its ties and its emotions, must today be one of the fundamental bases of our external activities.

Of course, we did not fail to tell the Arabs that for us the State of Israel was a *fait accompli* and that we would not permit its destruction. So that, all things considered, one might have imagined that a day would come when our country could help directly in concluding and guaranteeing a real peace in the East, provided no fresh drama arose to sunder it.

But, alas, the drama did arise.

It had been led up to by a very grave and constant tension, resulting from the scandalous lot of the refugees in Jordan and from the threats of destruction freely made against Israel. On

May 22, the vexatious affair of Aqaba, created by Egypt, was to offer a pretext to those who had been longing to come to blows. In order to avert hostilities, France proposed to the other three Powers on May 24 that they should, in conjunction with her, forbid either of the two sides to start any fighting.

On June 2, the French government stated officially that in the event it would lay the blame on whoever initiated any military action and this is what it repeated quite clearly to all the countries involved. This is what I had myself stated to Mr Eban, the Israeli Foreign Minister, when I saw him in Paris on May 24. If Israel is attacked, I said to him in effect, we shall not allow you to be destroyed, but if you attack we shall condemn your initiative. Despite your inferiority in numbers of population, it must be granted that you are much better organized, much more united and much better armed than the Arabs, and I do not doubt that should the occasion arise your arms will be successful. But then you would find yourselves involved in increasing difficulties both on the ground and from the international point of view; especially since war in the East cannot fail to increase the deplorable tension in the world and have very unwelcome consequences in many countries. So that if you become conquerors the disadvantages that result will come to be blamed on you.

We know that France's voice was not heeded. Israel attacked and in six days of fighting seized the objectives she wanted. Now, in the territories she has captured, she is organizing an occupation which can but be accompanied by oppression, repression and expulsion; and the resistance which is being displayed there she, in her turn, calls terrorism. It is true that for a the time being the two belligerents are observing, in a precarious and irregular fashion, the cease-fire laid down by the United Nations.

But the conflict has only been interrupted and there cannot, therefore, be any solution to it except by international means. Unless the United Nations tear up their own charter, any such settlement must be based on the evacuation of the territories seized by force, on an end to all warlike activities, and on the recognition by all the countries involved of each other.

After which, through decisions at the United Nations and with the presence of UN troops as a safeguard, it would probably be possible to settle the exact line of the frontiers, the conditions of life and security on both sides, the fate of the refugees and minorities, and the terms for opening the Gulf of Aqaba and the

Suez Canal to all shipping. An agreement between the Great Powers, entailing, *ipso facto*, agreement at the United Nations, is of course necessary, *would* be necessary, if such a settlement is to be got under way, or if any settlement at all and especially the one outlined is to come to pass, a settlement to which, what is more, according to France, there should be added an international statute for Jerusalem; if such an agreement were to come to pass France is prepared in advance to lend her political, economic and military aid so that it may be effectively implemented.

But we do not see how any agreement at all can be born until such time as one of the Four Powers has extricated itself from the hateful war it is waging elsewhere, for everything in the world today is related to everything else. But for the war in Vietnam, the conflict between Israel and the Arabs would not have become what it is, and if peace was to come again to South-East Asia, it would come also to the Middle East, thanks to the general détente that would follow such an event.

Here is the passage about Canada, from the same press conference:

It was the French who, more than two and a half centuries ago and up until 1763, discovered, settled and administered Canada. When, 204 years ago, the king's government, which had suffered serious reverses on the Continent and could not, in consequence, keep the war going against England in America, felt that it must abandon the territory, sixty thousand Frenchmen were settled in the St Lawrence Basin. Subsequently, their community has received only infinitesimal reinforcement from that of metropolitan France. And this while millions upon millions of British immigrants, relieved more recently by new arrivals, Slavs, Mediterraneans, Scandinavians, Jews and Asiatics whom the Canadian government in Ottawa has been determined to anglicize, have settled throughout the country.

Here, finally, is the main part of the Jesuit Father Michel Riquet's article, entitled 'Between Israel and Ishmael' which appeared in the *Figaro* on December 6, 1967:

The bruised hearts of our Israelite friends have been painfully affected by General de Gaulle's remarks on the Middle East situation. Some indeed have felt that they were an insult and a betrayal. What bitter derision for the survivors of Auschwitz and Treblinka to find the purposes and practices of their executioners being attributed to them!

But although we can understand the passionate reactions of the Jewish soul in such circumstances, the very friendship and the profound sympathy which we keep for it make it our duty not to allow a misunderstanding harmful to those very people whose cause is dear to us to grow worse.

When I re-read the text of the famous speech I must confess I find in it the undeniable gift of the author of the *Salvation: War Memoirs* for portraying dramatic situations in bold strokes and for recreating the sequence of a series of events. His analysis of the basic psychological facts implied in the birth of the State of Israel cannot seriously be questioned. It is perfectly accurate that just after the first world war the creation of a home for Zionists in Palestine aroused, even among Israel's friends and even among more than one devout Israelite, 'a certain amount of apprehension'. By recalling the opinions that were current at that time, prior to Hitler, General de Gaulle is not putting forward anything that is not historical when he says: 'Some even feared that the Jews, scattered hitherto but who had remained what they had always been, that is an élite people, self-assured and domineering, might, once they were reunited, turn the very moving hopes they had formed over nineteen centuries: "Next year in Jerusalem", into a burning ambition of conquest.' These fears, as we know, were belied by the peaceful activities which caused the desert to bloom again. But this does not mean that 'some people' could not have them and did not have them. Nothing permits us to assert that the General is underwriting them himself.

*　　*　　*

The Jews are especially sensitive about the term 'domineering' because this immediately reminds them of the Protocols of the Elders of Zion and the obsessions of the anti-semites. Xavier Vallat, for example, the Commissioner for Jewish Affairs under the Vichy regime, wrote the following lines in April 1942 in the magazine *La Légion*: 'The Jew is a foreigner who is not content simply to want to live on the soil he has adopted momentarily; his natural rights as a member of a superior race, made to dominate the world, make him want to rule it.'

General de Gaulle's diplomacy has hardened with regard to Israel; the partial embargo on the fifty Mirage fighters was followed in January 1969 by a total embargo. This decision was made known to the press, accompanied by a little phrase about 'Israeli influence among influential figures in the news media' which also provoked various reactions.

I continue to believe that General de Gaulle is acting in accordance with the usages of 'power politics', inspired purely and simply by France's interests as conceived by him.

In his book *Prélude à Suez*, the former Israeli Ambassador to France recounts the two conversations he had with General de Gaulle on April 28, 1955. From it I have taken the following extracts:

He told me he still could not see a single stable régime in any of the Arab countries. Ever since the dawn of their history, the Arabs had always been divided and subject to innumerable dissensions. Any attempt to unite them was doomed to failure.

The English having failed at it time and again in the past thirty years, who could be expected to succeed? One only needed to look at what the Arab League had been reduced to. Was there any reason to predict a different fate for the pacts and alliances that the Arabs were trying to set up in our own day? What had changed in the meantime? The fact that oil had been discovered in their subsoil and that they had as a consequence millions of dollars at their disposal!

De Gaulle told me that he considered the creation of the Jewish State as a historical necessity. The Jewish people had the right to expect reparation for the historical injustice of which it had been the victim for centuries past. Moreover, who had ever established the right of the Arabs to the *whole* Middle East, to the exclusion of all foreign elements? There had never been a united Arab Kingdom in that part of the world since the decline of the Caliphate, which in any case had existed only ephemerally. The Arab States had been created artificially after the first world war. Throughout their history the Arabs had always been subject to foreign domination. One after the other, the Romans, the Byzantines, the Mamelukes and the Turks had been their masters. In the name of what principles were they now claiming the domination of the whole Eastern Mediterranean?

The creation of Israel and its rapid development had pleasantly surprised him, the General assured me. He had always been able to appreciate the gifts of the Jews, their clear and logical minds and their energy. But he would never have imagined them being so successful at agriculture. He had been able himself to observe their progress on the land on his frequent visits to Palestine during the war, and he had continued to follow it closely since.

He spoke to me admiringly about the organisation of the Israeli army and its excellence in combat. General de Gaulle considered the Israeli army to be a highly significant military formation, perfectly capable of taking on the Arab armies. He checked himself, however, and told me:

'You must understand me aright: you will have for all that to face long years of border incidents, acts of sabotage and frantic agitation. However much I think about it, it is hard to find a quick solution that would put an end to the conflict between Israel and her neighbours. But I do not see any immediate danger that might threaten your existence. Your presence in the Middle East is a reality, and no doctrine can ignore that. What is more, the world political situation will finally convince the Great Powers that it is vital to ensure Israel's existence in that area.'

During our talk, General de Gaulle made it clear that Israel would have to amend her frontiers – including Jerusalem – 'and above all you will be forced to guarantee yourselves free egress to the Red Sea, even if it means a war'.

Was there any such thing as a French policy these days? For various historical reasons, he said, France had not had an independent foreign policy for 150 years. (Some rapid mental arithmetic took me back to the Napoleonic era.) The internal weaknesses of the régime had led to conformism and a lack of initiative, and there was very little chance of this situation changing in the near future.

But if one day – and he hoped this day would come – there was room once more for such a policy in the conduct of the nation's affairs, its repercussions in the Middle East would soon make themselves felt. In that part of the world France would have to depend on all the ethnic and religious minorities in order to counteract the exclusive domination of the Muslim majority. That was the natural tendency of French policy, which had lent its support in the past to the Maronites, the Armenians and the Kurds. Support of Israel was a part of this political doctrine, for the Jewish State, simply because it exists, forms an 'important reference-point in the present constellation in the Middle East'.

Here are the General's remarks after the Sinai campaign, as reported by the Ambassador:

Tell Ben Gurion that even if, this time, he has to give up Sinai, Israel will have derived much profit from the campaign. Her international position and her role in the Middle East have changed completely. The Israeli army has won a brilliant victory. Even if circumstances force her to withdraw she will never lose the prestige conferred on her by the battle of Sinai. From now on, Israel has consolidated her position in the area. However difficult the political struggle you will have to sustain, that is an advantage which can but have its effect on the future destiny of the Middle East.

* * *

The sole object of these excerpts is to provide a basis for the interpretation of General de Gaulle's diplomacy which I am putting forward: in 1955 he was thinking of a move aimed at strengthening the non-Arab or non-Muslim minorities in the area, today he is backing the Arabs, not because he is anti-Zionist or still less anti-semitic, but in the interests of France.

In his own eyes, General de Gaulle is the embodiment of France and he gets irritated when numbers of Frenchmen oppose him and, either emotionally or rationally, criticize what he says or does. Those Frenchmen who are Jews either by faith or simply by origin probably play a disproportionate part in the opposition to his Middle East policy. They thereby become suspected of a 'double allegiance', at a time when Jewish students and teachers are marching in the forefront of the rebels at Columbia, Nanterre or the Sorbonne. In Israel, it is true, students do three years' national service before going to university, and do not rebel.

Part 1
The Press Conference

The Press Conference

The recent meeting between the Chief Rabbi and General de Gaulle, and the latter's letter to Mr Ben Gurion call for a brief comment but not, it seems to me, any amendment to the text which follows. In connection with the phrase which provoked so much emotion, 'an élite people, self-assured and domineering', the President of the Republic now assures us that 'there can be nothing unkind in emphasizing the characteristic that has enabled this steadfast people to survive and to remain itself through nineteen centuries passed in conditions without parallel.'

The anonymous letters received the day after the Press Conference would be sufficient proof, if the evidence required proof, that Frenchmen (M. Xavier Vallat in particular) did not all interpret this phrase, inserted into a lengthy exposition on Israel, as being a panegyric of the Jewish people. Like many of our Head of State's phrases this one is wilfully ambiguous. Moreover, to call the people of the ghettoes 'self-assured and domineering' still seems to me today to be as ludicrous as it is hateful.

The fact remains though – and I am delighted he should have done so – that General de Gaulle, without retracting anything of what he said or toning down his condemnation of the policy of the Israeli government, has sought to deny the charges of anti-semitism levelled at him. I shall not underwrite these charges in the pages that follow for the very notion of anti-semitism is endlessly ambiguous. The Press Conference solemnly *authorized* a new form of anti-semitism; the Head of State's subsequent remarks suspend this authorization, so to speak, but in the true style of the *Prince*, in other words by shifting his own responsibility on to others: only 'systematic anti-Gaullists' (René Cassin for example) could 'pretend to interpret pejoratively' what any upright mind could see to be complimentary.

The last word has yet to be spoken. No one needs to be told any longer about the technique of blowing hot and cold, or about changes of heart. Two steps forward, one step back, then two steps forward again. In spite of everything I subscribe, willingly but without too many illusions, to André Fontaine's formula: 'It is not, therefore, too late to hope that a constructive dialogue will take the place of these futile and acrimonious polemics'.

The Age of Suspicion

Weeks and months have passed since General de Gaulle's Press Conference without making it any less actual. The President of the Republic's remarks continue to agitate 'the bruised hearts of our Israelite friends', as Father Riquet has written (*Figaro*, December 6, 1967). 'Passionate reactions of the Jewish soul', understandable but unjustified? 'A harmful misunderstanding' which the exegete, equipped with his generous sentiments and his subtlety, will contrive to clear up? No, Reverend Father. I do not doubt your sympathy, but I owe it to you to be frank and I would be failing in my obligation if I did not admit my 'passionate reaction' to your article. Why deny the evidence, and with such conviction? No one is obliged morally to take sides; after all, many others who should have heard, heard nothing. You heard and then you decided to re-read the speech. Well, let us re-read it together. After all, laymen are not ignorant or disrespectful of the rules of exegesis. No one will dare to suspect General de Gaulle of indulging in the delights of improvisation. Now three parenthetical clauses reveal the speaker's deliberately aggressive intent.

'One might have asked oneself, and even many Jews have asked themselves, whether the planting of this community in lands acquired under more or less justifiable conditions and in the midst of Arab populations fundamentally hostile to it, would not lead to ceaseless and interminable friction and conflict.' Such questions were indeed asked, and rightly. One might also ask oneself whether the President of the Republic considers it useful to his diplomacy and consistent with the interests of France to go back over the past and give us his own account of the events leading up to the birth of the State of Israel. The expression 'more or less justifiable' to qualify the acquisition of territory offended the Israelis; it settles, in favour of the Arabs, one of the issues that has been argued over in vain for many years. But many Jews have indeed rejected Zionism not only because they wanted to be Frenchmen, Germans or Americans, but also because they foresaw an interminable war between the two communities, the Jewish and the Arab, in Palestine.

Let us read the following sentence together, Reverend Father: 'Some even feared that the Jews, scattered hitherto but who had remained what they had always been, that is an élite people, self-assured and domineering, might, once they were reunited, turn the very moving hopes they had formed over nineteen centuries: "Next year in Jerusalem", into a burning ambition of conquest.' Your commentary is worth its weight in gold: according to you, 'these fears were belied by the peaceful activities which caused the desert to bloom again' – which does not mean that certain people did not have these fears and that 'nothing permits us to assert that the General is underwriting them himself.'

Did 'certain people' feel these fears in advance? Maybe: how can it be proved that these 'certain people' did not exist? But when one remembers the image of the Jew portrayed by anti-semites – the Jew with his bent back and his grasping fingers – 'one might have asked oneself' how many people foresaw and feared the military exploits of the Israelis. Moreover, it matters little whether or not General de Gaulle has underwritten 'certain people's fears'. The words which 'stirred the bruised hearts' – to wit the Jews 'hitherto scattered, but who had remained what they had always been, an élite people, self-assured and domineering' – were not attributed to anyone; it was General de Gaulle who qualified the Jewish people as 'self-assured and domineering.' Defining a 'people' by two adjectives: a statesman demeans himself when he resorts to national stereotypes and racial prejudice. General de Gaulle demeaned himself because he wanted to hit below the belt, to explain Israeli imperialism by the eternal nature and domineering instinct of the Jewish people. Why this low blow? That I don't know. But for heaven's sake, Father, you must admit that there is something to be understood, even for someone who, as a non-Jew, does not have a bruised heart.

The phrase concerning the Jewish people, 'self-assured and domineering', did not answer in any way the requirements of the General's proof. Whether or not the Jews constitute a people and whether or not they are domineering, the setting up of a home for Jews in Palestine indeed risked, perhaps even led inexorably to interminable conflict. And the dialectic of hostility in its turn may have incited the Israelis to aggression. But this does not mean that the Jewish people, by its nature and throughout the centuries, is and remains 'self-assured and domineering'.

A little further on, a correction of General de Gaulle by himself betrays if not the sentiments of the speaker then at least the intentions of the politician. Must it be said that the Jews 'provoked' or 'aroused' 'ill-feeling' (what an admirable euphemism!). The President of the Republic is not going to let anyone be mistaken about that. Let us read him together, Reverend Father: 'In spite of the wave of ill-feeling, now rising, now falling, which they provoked, or rather aroused, in certain countries and at certain times, a considerable capital of interest and even sympathy had accrued in their favour, especially, it must be said, in Christendom'.

Once again one must admire the artistry of the Prince. We have known for a long time of course that it is the persecuted who are responsible for their persecution. As for the capital sum of interest and sympathy for the Jews that has accrued in Christendom, may I suggest to the President of the Republic that he read some books on the history of anti-semitism? The inculcation of contempt, the pogroms in the Rhineland on the eve of the First Crusade, twenty tragic centuries have been subsumed into a single piece of literary bravura which would call for nothing more than a shrug of the shoulders if the speaker had not summoned the whole world to witness to his genius.

And then the Jews turn up for a third time in the speech, among the invaders of Quebec. Among the 'new arrivals whom the Canadian government has been determined to anglicize', the Jews are given a place of honour among the Mediterraneans, the Slavs, the Scandinavians and the Asiatics. Once again the Jews qualify for a separate mention.

But, everyone, Jew and Christian alike, will say, has General de Gaulle not proved the absurdity of the charge of anti-semitism made against him by his actions? On many occasions

Jews had leading roles with the Free French, in the Gaullist mass-movement, the Rassemblement du Peuple Français, and in the Gaullist parliamentary party, the UNR General de Gaulle, the man whom Charles de Gaulle talks about in the third person, does not appear to have made any distinction between Jewish Frenchman and non-Jewish Frenchmen. Why should he repudiate his own handiwork, his past and his reputation? Why should he who wishes to embody France alienate not only the Jews but also those who have not forgotten the 'abominable persecutions' suffered by the Jews during the second world war, those who are still haunted by the memory of the gas-ovens and those, too, who quite simply think it futile not to say culpable to add one more conflict gratuitously to all the others that are rending the French nation.

These are fair questions, but they do not cancel out the facts: the Jews of France, or rather of the whole world, at once grasped the historic import of the few words uttered on November 28, 1967, by the President of the French Republic; the anti-semites (and M. Xavier Vallat did not hold back for a moment) had received solemn authorization from the Head of State to make themselves heard again and to employ the same language as before the Final Solution. National anti-semitism had once again become *salonfähig*, as the Germans put it. Now – and I defy any man of good faith to contradict me – General de Gaulle cannot have failed to foresee the passionate reactions which he 'provoked, or rather aroused'. No other Western statesman had talked about the Jews in this way, or characterized them as a 'people' by means of two adjectives. We all recognize the style and the adjectives as being those of Edouard Drumont and Charles Maurras,[1] not those of Hitler. After all, Bernanos never admitted that there was any connection at all between his old mentor, Maurras, to whom he remained loyal right up to the last, and Hitler, who filled him with a deep horror.

For the past twenty years, a sort of taboo has inhibited us from speaking freely on this subject. Some friend will tell me that the Jews had exercised a sort of terror: by evoking or invoking their dead they forbade any discussion of a problem that does not

[1] The more a 'domineering' people deserves the qualification of 'élite' the more fear it inspires, and the more it asks to be discriminated against.

cease to exist simply because its existence is denied. Indeed, it may happen that a problem is created by being posited. But let us admit that the problem exists. I had thought, in my naïvety, that a 'certain silence' could be explained not so much by Jewish terrorism as by scruples of conscience. What would a Drumont have thought if he had lived to witness the genocide? 'I didn't want this'? Or would his self-criticism have gone further?

Probably I was wrong. Let us leave the dead to bury the dead. No Jew ought to impose silence on the anti-semites by reminding them of former sufferings, however excessive. I am not going to liken the anti-semites of 1967 to Hitler, so as to disqualify them without hearing what they have to say. But, writing freely in a free country, I shall say that General de Gaulle has knowingly and deliberately initiated a new phase of Jewish history and perhaps of anti-semitism. Everything has once again become possible; everything is beginning over again. Agreed, there is no threat of persecution, only of 'ill-will'. It is not the age of contempt, but the age of suspicion.

And now to the argument, since argue we must.

*   *   *

During his bi-annual monologue, on November 27, 1967, General de Gaulle insisted, somewhat surprisingly at first sight, on treating at length of Israel and of Quebec. In neither case did the Press Conference reveal any noticeable change in his previous positions; both Israelis and Arabs knew which way General de Gaulle's sympathies were inclining or, to be more precise, on which side he had aligned himself. (Since the vote at the United Nations, the fiction of neutrality had been exploded.) As for the inhabitants of Quebec, they already knew (even if they did not all want to know) that General de Gaulle had recommended sovereignty, that is separatism, for them. But, for all its splendour, the Word cannot, at one fell swoop, create peace along the Suez Canal or in Jordan, nor the material conditions for political and economic independence along the banks of the St Lawrence.

The importance General de Gaulle has attached to these two

recent crises of his reign can hardly be explained by his will to influence the course of events. The settlement of the Arab-Israeli conflict which he outlined contains, skilfully blended, clauses that would be unacceptable to either one side or the other. It is no better and no worse than other plans, and has not the slightest chance of being accepted by either side in the present circumstances. In point of fact, it is not a peace settlement at all, but a settlement of accounts.

Whom with? With the French press which, twice in six months, had been guilty of *lèse-majesté*, having criticized the conduct of France's foreign policy and having alienated opinion, or a part of it, from the man who, since June 1940 if not earlier, had been the embodiment of French legitimacy and the embodiment of France itself. 'What would Valéry have said about our press if he had lived to read what so many of our papers managed to print on the occasion of General de Gaulle's visit to the Frenchmen of Canada.' In the Quebec affair the press got in between General de Gaulle and public opinion. In the Middle East affair it is the Jews who have intervened. The interpreters of the Elysée Palace have made sure that we know what 'talking meant'. The Jews, having come together in Palestine and henceforth constituting the nation of Israel, have embarked on the path of conquest. The Jews of the diaspora must choose between their own countries and Israel. They must indeed choose, and the vast majority of French Jews chose, without hesitation or reservation, France. But will they ever manage to rid themselves of their old 'self-assured and domineering' nature, if they have not done so after twenty centuries? Are they going to lose the right to feel and to show sympathy for the State of Israel just because they are French citizens?

We must go cautiously at this point and not fall into the trap that has been laid for us. By inserting a phrase about the 'Jewish people' into a historical disquisition on the birth of Israel, the Head of State was deliberately calling for two responses, one defending the state of Israel, the other denouncing his summary not to say insulting qualification of the Jews *qua* Jews. The conjunction of these two responses would give fresh foundation to the implicit accusation of double allegiance. The Jews would inevitably be split, some being anxious simply to assert with renewed force their single and exclusive allegiance to France, while others would be inclined to claim the right simultaneously to French citizenship and sympathy for Israel; thus, each would accuse the other either of harbouring anti-semitism or of betraying their 'Jewishness'. They would be guilty if they did not accept unblinkingly the about-turn in the national interest (as interpreted by General de Gaulle), and guilty also if they did, being thus condemned to betray either their country or their brothers.

Let us try, however, to separate out what the machiavellianism of one man plus twenty centuries of history have tended to confound inextricably. In France, under the Fifth Republic, any Frenchman, Jew or non-Jew, has the right, in accordance with the constitution, to comment freely on the utterances and actions of the President of the Republic. To criticize the Head of State is not the same as insulting him.

I have never believed in the permanence of the exclusive alliance between France and Israel in the Middle East. It originated in the struggle waged by France in North Africa to preserve her sovereignty there, and threatened not to outlive the conditions that had brought it into being. Those who can see international relations for what they are need feign neither astonishment nor indignation when the calculations of the 'cold-blooded monsters' turn enemies into allies and allies into enemies. When Mr Ben Gurion visited Paris Israel was still a friend and an ally and yet, according to General de Gaulle in 1967, 'thanks to the Franco-British expedition to Suez . . . we watched the emergence of a State of Israel that was warlike and set on expansion.' One may well wonder whether, even in terms of the national interest, it would not have been better to have carried out this about-turn, so consistent with the unwritten laws of the international jungle, in a less provocative manner.

After all, teachers of machiavellianism have never counselled Princes to show too many outward signs of cynicism. Simple mortals whose insignificance removes them from the Elysian heights do not live in accordance with the imperatives of power politics, they have feelings that are both naïve and primitive, they like to think that the man guiding them belongs to the same humanity as themselves, that he takes the national interest into account but also certain imponderables, as they say, justice and suffering . . .

But enough. Jews may suffer from the breaking-off of the pact between France and Israel, which had made it simple for them to be French citizens of Jewish origin.[1] They may regret it and argue the advantages and disadvantages on the selfsame plane where the Head of State has quite rightly taken his stand, that of the national interest. *Qua* State, Israel, so original in many respects, is a State just like any other, not a just State but a violent one, threatened with extinction and constrained to use force in order to survive. Friendship between monsters does not last.

Moreover, the Jews of France, including those who volunteered for Israel (often passionate Gaullists) found it easy to understand France's neutrality between the Arab countries and Israel. After Algerian independence and the carrying through of decolonization any French government would have striven to re-establish the so-called traditional ties with the Arab countries of the Middle East. General de Gaulle strove to do so, with success, without thereby coming out against Israel. It was probably his ambition, and a noble one too, to help to reconcile 'Israel and Ishmael'. And according to my information he believed himself to be on the verge of success. The violence of his remarks may therefore have expressed a disappointment commensurate with his earlier hopes.

Of course, he blames others. Let us go back to the crisis of May and June 1967. France's interests, those of the Arab countries, those of Israel itself (whatever the Israelis may now think) demanded above all that they should avoid a war which some on both sides probably wanted but which would only be one episode in a prolonged conflict and would not, in any case, solve a thing. To anyone who knew the situation in the Middle East, the closing of the Gulf of Aqaba made war seem extremely probable. The Egyptians knew this as well as the Israelis. And now 'the vexatious affair of Aqaba, created by Egypt' (delightful euphemism) has become 'a pretext to those who had been long-

---

[1] I use this term for want of a better one to denote those Jews among whom I class myself, who are neither religious nor practising, and who have not even preserved anything of 'Jewish culture'.

ing to come to blows'. At the time, I happened to have dinner with a minister who had just come from a cabinet meeting at the Elysée Palace and proved to me with trade statistics that after all the 'affair' was of no importance. I tried in vain to persuade him to the contrary. If General de Gaulle had used his influence with President Nasser to turn him back from this venture, if, either on his own or in agreement with the United States and Great Britain, he had honoured the commitment entered into by the government of the Fourth Republic to keep the Gulf of Aqaba open to shipping, the Six Day War would not have taken place. Admittedly, General de Gaulle would not then have been able to glory in his useless and solitary wisdom. Effective action would have replaced the glories of language.

French diplomacy made the same mistake as that of Yugoslavia and India: the delegates of these two countries to the United Nations pushed U Thant into giving satisfaction to President Nasser as quickly as possible, that is into withdrawing the peace-keeping force, and thereby setting the infernal machine in motion. In the same way, General de Gaulle did nothing to prevent the blockade of the Gulf of Aqaba, the build-up of Egyptian troops in Sinai, the alliance between Jordan and Syria, the entry of Iraqi troops into Jordan – in other words, the events that inexorably brought about the explosion. He proposed a four-power conference which the Russians rejected (this should not have surprised him) and he finally resolved, for want of anything better, solemnly to condemn, in advance and from an Olympian height, the side that fired the first shot. One glance at a map would have shown, without great risk of error, which side, logically, had to fire the first shot. From that day on, France had renounced her neutrality and had taken sides: the Israelis were guilty of the crime of *lèse-gaullisme* they preferred the safety of their towns to the tokens of compassion and esteem which General de Gaulle had promised them, at his next press conference, as repayment for their docility. If he had been in Mr Levi Eshkol's shoes the author of the *The Edge of the Sword* would have behaved just as he did.

Passive when he may still have had a chance of averting the conflict, verbally aggressive when there was no longer anything he could do, General de Gaulle added to his other feats by a few timely words: the day before Messrs Kosygin and Johnson met in Glassboro he declared that because of the Vietnam war the Russians and Americans were no longer on speaking terms. (In point of fact, the hot line had been in action since the morning of June 5, 1967, and the two Great Powers had agreed on non-intervention.) At the first session of the United Nations after the crisis, the French delegation increased its efforts, with limited success, to rally the French-speaking States of Africa to the Russian motion.

Gaullists will tell me that this was dictated by the national interest. Sympathy or antipathy matter little. Reconciled with the Arab world France could not lose the opportunity to strengthen the ties which even the Algerian war had not completely broken. If she remained neutral France would not have differentiated herself sufficiently from the United States and Great Britain. The prior condemnation of whoever fired the first shot was a stroke of genius: it created the impression of neutrality while in fact making neutrality impossible. It shook French public opinion, which was pro-Israeli for the most part but also in favour of peace.

Maybe so, and once the decision to side with the Arab countries has been allowed it is hard to see any better pretext (although one can but smile at the President of the Republic deciding what is just and unjust and giving orders to sovereign States). But had this decision been taken before the declaration committing France? Can General de Gaulle's irritation against Israel not be explained, at least in part, by the illusions he had harboured over the power of his prohibitions, illusions that may have been shared by his new 'allies and friends' in Cairo and Damascus?

So far as I can judge, General de Gaulle did not foresee either the consequences of the 'vexatious affair' at Aqaba, nor the speed of the Israeli victory. To his visitors from Israel, he declared the need for an agreement between the Four Powers or, to be more precise still, the urgency of negotiating with the Soviet Union: he linked the Israel crisis with the war in Vietnam. The Israeli diplomats for their part wondered what miracle General de Gaulle was counting on to convert the rulers of the Kremlin to the idea of a peaceful settlement. They could hardly

believe de Gaulle's thesis that the Russians were carrying out a
diversionary operation in the Middle East in answer to American
aggression in Vietnam. Insofar as they took this hypothesis at
all seriously, they questioned themselves with even greater
anxiety about the chances and advantages of a negotiation
between the Four Powers. Nothing can be done without the
participation of the Russians, General de Gaulle repeated. All
right, but what can be done with that participation? replied the
Israelis.

The balance-sheet for France of de Gaulle's diplomacy between
May and November 28, 1967, has yet to be drawn up. No one
could honestly claim that the gains and losses can be measured
objectively. The gratitude of the Arab countries, the disappointment of the Israelis: everyone will weigh up these immaterial
assets on his own particular scales. Millions of men who
harboured a 'certain idea of France' have gone into mourning
for their affection. In August, 1967 an Israeli minister said to me:
'We felt no fear, so long as that gallant knight General de Gaulle
remains in power we can count on France.' I told him: 'Your
mistake was to confuse Saint Louis with Louis xi.' But millions
of other men have rediscovered or think they have rediscovered
their France.

There was nothing *making* General de Gaulle choose. Before
May, 1967, he was the one western Head of State to inspire confidence in both camps. And now he too can only speak to one of
them. Even for President Nasser a General de Gaulle who was
persona grata in Washington and Jerusalem would have been more
valuable than one modelling himself on Marshal Tito. In order
to obtain what he has indeed obtained there was no need for the
French President to lose what he will never win back. Deceit-
fulness in the service of some great undertaking is easily forgiven
and sometimes even evokes admiration; but not when the
objective smells of petrol and when the turnabout seems to have
been dictated by bad temper, wounded pride or some obscure
piece of calculation.

*　　*　　*

'You are forgetting the essential', someone of good will (not
necessarily a Gaullist) will object. 'You are pointing out the

turnabout in alliances without taking into account the turnabout in values. Since June 1967, Israel has no longer looked to the world like David facing Goliath, a small nation surrounded by enemies eager for its destruction, but as a proud nation, with its foot on the necks of a million Arabs. Once again, General de Gaulle realized before others which way the immediate future would go. Opinion in Europe and perhaps even in America, will make Israel pay dearly for its earlier enthusiasm and its present disillusionment.'

According to the Press Conference of November 27, 1967, Israel had appeared as a warlike State set on expansion ever since 1956. Several years later, when Mr Ben Gurion visited Paris, General de Gaulle was still referring to the country represented by his guest as 'friend and ally'. He continued to sell arms to it. Everyone was aware that the recluse of Colombey had blamed the failure of the Suez expedition on the incompetent régime of the Fourth Republic, he had never condemned its principle or its immorality. If General de Gaulle really thought that Israel 'would be led to expand her territory whenever an opportunity arose' why did he go on selling Mystères and Mirages to her? Unless, in accordance with the Israeli version of the talks between Ben Gurion and de Gaulle, the French President looked favourably or even advised his interlocutor on the territorial expansion he now condemns. General MacArthur too, when he got back from Korea, proclaimed naïvely in front of the entire United States Congress, that Japan and China had changed sides, Japan going from bad to good and China following the same course in the opposite direction. No one is going to charge de Gaulle with being naïve. For him, it is the national interest that matters.

But for us? I am ready to answer this. Israel compromised her cause by associating herself with the Franco-British expedition of 1956 against Egypt. With determination she took advantage of the final spasm of Franco-British imperialism to teach Egypt a lesson, to put a stop to the *fedayin* raids and to open up Eilat to shipping. Did the advantages balance out the moral cost of this venture, which the secret collusion with Sir Anthony Eden and M. Guy Mollet had made quite unacceptable to the best, to the true friends of Israel? That is for the Israelis themselves to decide, I shall not claim to settle this question in the name of the conscience of mankind. As a French citizen I disapproved of the whole undertaking for reasons that were as much moral as political: the occupation of the Suez Canal or even the fall of President Nasser would not have restored peace either in Algeria or in the Middle East. Cynicism is no guarantee of effectiveness.

Some people are now seeking to rehabilitate what is best forgotten by invoking the events of 1967. If the United States had allowed the French and British to go ahead, they tell us, or if the latter, despite Russian and American opposition, had had the courage to go through with it, the world would have been spared a war. I am not going to go back over the preliminaries to the aggression of the Israelis, the British and the French or over their respective responsibility. I feel scarcely any more indulgent towards John Foster Dulles than I do towards Sir Anthony Eden. But, in the last resort, those who take a decision to resort to armed force should at least work out the balance of forces and foresee the probable reactions of the various actors. The American reaction to a twentieth-century brand of gunboat diplomacy was at least probable. And what Egyptian government would have followed President Nasser's after the withdrawal of the French and British troops (supposing that these had occupied the Canal Zone for a few months)? In 1956 the French, deliberately, and the British, without wanting to, lent aid and assistance to the State of Israel. The rulers of this State adjudged that, situated as they were, they must forego the luxury of moral scruples. Eleven years later, I still cannot resign myself to saying they were right.

My commitment with regard to France and my feelings with regard to Israel did not change between 1956 and 1967. The switching of alliances did not surprise me, although it was carried out in a gratuitously aggressive manner. I shall leave aside the assessment of profit and loss, since this must by its nature be uncertain, and restrict myself to the analysis of the interpretation which General de Gaulle proposes of the crisis of June, 1967. This interpretation seems to me profoundly unjust or, rather, deliberately inaccurate.

To present the Aqaba affair as a 'pretext' for those who were longing to come to blows, is to distort the facts: the Israeli government had proclaimed many times that it would not stand

2

for the closing of the Gulf of Aqaba while the Suez Canal remained out of bounds to Israeli shipping. Nothing in the present state of our knowledge authorizes us to portray the State of Israel as watching for the opportunity to conquer. Certainly there existed men or groups who were hoping for such an opportunity. The government in power, that of Mr Levi Eshkol, represented the opposite faction. On the very day when hostilities were unleashed the Prime Minister disclaimed all territorial ambition.

I want it to be understood that I am not trying to substitute one simple-minded picture for another. The Israelis are not angels any more than the Arabs are monsters (or vice versa). Both are confronted in an inexpiable conflict which they tend more and more to see as inexpiable. In April, 1967, neither the Israelis nor President Nasser wanted or were preparing for war. The permanent tension grew progressively worse, Israeli reprisals answered attacks by terrorists, the 'progressives' in Syria made President Nasser feel ashamed of his passivity. When States will not accept each other mutually and maintain an insecurity verging on open hostility along their frontiers, I admire those who claim, from afar, to decide on justice and injustice, on 'legitimate reprisals' and 'excessive brutality'. To men of goodwill everything in the Middle East seemed shocking, the fate of the refugees of course, as General de Gaulle said, but also the shelling of kibbutzim by Syrian artillery, the inculcation of hatred in all Arab schools, the threats of annihilation made against a State recognized by the international community.

One could go on listing such abuses indefinitely, but the fact remains that in May, 1967, the initiatives which carried the war within them 'as the storm-clouds carry the storm' came from President Nasser. By closing the Gulf of Aqaba he not only defied Israel but also the United States and Great Britain. At the same time he was defying France, since she too, in 1957, had solemnly pledged herself towards Israel; he had probably been reassured previously on this point by the representatives of General de Gaulle. This defiance does not by itself prove that President Nasser 'wanted' war. When it sent an ultimatum to Serbia and ordered the shelling of Belgrade, the Austro-Hungarian government likewise was challenging Europe. It probably did not want a war, and certainly not the war that ensued. Perhaps President Nasser would have been satisfied by the diplomatic success which the closure of the Gulf of Aqaba represented after the withdrawal of the United Nations peace-keeping force. But he was well aware – and his mouthpiece put it in writing–that he had brought Israel to bay, so to speak. And he reckoned that even if he did not win the ensuing war decisively then at least he would not lose it. Now, Egypt only needed to keep going for a few days in an even battle to win a victory which would, in the long run, condemn Israel to death.

Do I hear someone say that the Egyptian leader cannot have harboured aggressive designs, given the balance of forces as it was revealed on the battlefield? The objection does not stand up. Go and ask those who talked to General de Gaulle about the course of events that he foresaw after the inital successes of the Israelis. In Jerusalem, Mr Ben Gurion was weighed down and could see no hope either in resigning himself to surrender or in running the risk of an attack. The cabinet could not bring itself to take the Air Force generals at their word, and the generals themselves could still not convince their colleagues in the other services.

At the end of May, 1967, as challenge succeeded challenge and mobilization succeeded mobilization, the trial of arms became inevitable. I thought at the time and still do think that the Israeli government had no real choice any longer and that, in this situation, the major responsibility lay with its enemies. General de Gaulle had promised to intervene if Israel should find herself in danger of extinction. And, so M. Gorse informs us, a promise from General de Gaulle means something.[1] What help would he have sent to Israel, apart from a press conference?

Such, in the late Spring of 1967, were the feelings of the majority of Frenchmen and of the majority of Europeans (in Socialist Europe too, despite the attitudes of their governments). As time passed, these feelings probably lost something of their freshness and simplicity. People had feared for their destruction of a State, the extermination of a nation. And then this nation, come from a scattered 'people' which, over the centuries, had endured every form of persecution and finally survived it, suddenly won a brilliant victory and, having saved its life, was in

[1] M. Gorse is a former Minister of Information in the French Government.

danger of losing its soul. The Israeli soldiers were transformed into occupying forces.

And now everyone is asking the questions which no one asked himself in the emotion of the moment. Has Israeli propaganda mobilized opinion? Did it denounce a fictive danger of extermination simply in order to attain its objectives of conquest?

It was the Arabs who undertook pro-Israeli 'propaganda'. After the event, the threats of the Palestinian liberation front sound very hollow. They are no longer to be heard or, rather, the sound of them has been lost in the din of the tanks and the sands of the desert, that desert over which the Egyptian soldiers made their way, haggard and drunk with thirst and the sun, having been promised victory and a meeting-up with their Syrian comrades in Tel Aviv amidst the delights of massacre and looting. We may consider *now* that our earlier emotions were excessive, but – I speak for myself – we do not disown them. In Europe and in America, in Warsaw and in Paris, they were shared by millions, both Jews and non-Jews. But – and I ask pardon of my Arab friends in Tunisia, Algeria, Morocco and Egypt too (for I do not believe I have lost their friendship) – we were wrong about the military capabilities of the Egyptians, the Jordanians and the Syrians, but we were not wrong about the fate of the Israeli nation if it were defeated nor about the fate that awaits it tomorrow if it loses one battle. The Arabs can lose battle after battle but still win the war in the end (they have time, space and numbers on their side), Israel would lose both the war and her life if she lost a single battle. David brought down Goliath for a third time, but he is still David, momentarily superior thanks to what we now call intelligence and technological proficiency; afterwards, as before, he is without reserves and without anywhere he can retreat to. The besieged garrison has brought off a successful sally and enlarged its defensive perimeter. But it is still besieged and will go on being so for years, if not decades.

Was there not something ambiguous and, in certain circumstances, unpleasant about the pro-Israeli enthusiasm of June, 1967, a very dear friend asks me? 'Indecent demonstrations' decreed a contributor to the 'Tribune Libre' column of *Le Monde* which one had not thought to be an arbiter of decency. I agree; I did not like the bands of youngsters marching up the Champs-

Elysées shouting 'Israel will win', or the crowds in front of the Israeli embassy. I did not like the supporters of a French Algeria or the ones nostalgic for the Suez expedition who pursued their war against the Arabs vicariously through Israel. The best and the worst are carried along together by collective emotions; those who today set themselves up as judges of political morality have not always displayed a subtle sense of nuance. Never mind, let us accept the censure of those men who, in June, 1967, preserved their sang-froid throughout, and never felt the slightest uneasiness for the lives of the people of Israel or who, armed with statistics, compared the two and a half million Jews gathered in Palestine to the tens of millions of Indians who have just enough to eat to stop them dying of starvation. Those Frenchmen, Jew and non-Jew alike, who felt themselves concerned in the very depths of their being by the fate of so small a number in the Spring of 1967, do not need to apologize for their particular affinity. Should they be asking forgiveness? Who in France felt 'concerned' over the confrontation between India and Pakistan? The confrontation between Israel and the Arabs upset millions of Frenchmen and Englishmen, Germans and Russians, and not because of any 'Jewish plot' or because of the activities of Jewish Frenchmen (or French Jews) talking on the radio or writing in the papers (my friend Yves Cau, the *Figaro* correspondent in Israel, found it harder to resist his emotions than I did). In a civilization nurtured on Christianity, how could the fate of the nation where Christ was born fail to stir in everyone, believer or unbeliever, childhood memories and mixed feelings? For century after century the people that had not recognized the Saviour became the Christ among nations, its face covered with spittle. This was the nation which Voltaire, yes Voltaire, accused of giving off an odour intolerable to Christian nostrils . . . until the day when the smoke rose up from the factories of death in the Germany of Mendelssohn and Nietzsche.

All right, some man of good faith will object, I can understand that Christian Europe which, for the past twenty years, has been trying to forget rather than understand, should have rid itself of its guilty conscience in this way by denouncing in advance the genocide by which it believed, wrongly, the Israelis to be threatened. But shouldn't French Jews, those who, like yourself, state they are and want to be French citizens 'just like anyone else', and those too who chose France rather than Israel when they were repatriated from North Africa, shouldn't you have kept yourselves in the background, and avoided saying or doing anything that laid you open to charges of 'double allegiance'? What took place, during those days of madness, made inevitable the reversal of which General de Gaulle was less the instigator than the interpreter.

Of course, brother, like all men you are so sensible when you speak on behalf of other people. It would have been better if . . . the Jews should not have . . . All that goes without saying. I admit it, after the sunshine of June I was waiting for the hoarfrost of November. But the same people who shared in the pro-Israeli enthusiasm in the Spring, tended in the Autumn to harbour a resentment against the Jews for the feelings which they, who were not Jews, had felt. The major fact is forgotten which alone can explain the almost complete unanimity among Jews in France: because the sympathies of the majority of Frenchmen were with Israel the Jews felt an amazed joy, in the reconciliation of their French citizenship with their 'Jewishness'. By demonstrating their attachment to Israel they were not cutting themselves off from the French, but merging with them. It was too good to last, they too had been believing in Father Christmas.

A friend, like myself a 'de-judaized' Jew, has suggested one way out. Should the excesses of pro-Israelism, the 'indecent demonstrations', not be attributed to the new-comers, to the Jews who left North Africa after the Maghreb countries attained independence? The 'assimilated' ones on the other hand did not commit these errors of tact which quite rightly annoyed (the Head of State. This friend must forgive me, but his argument makes me feel ashamed. He brings back sinister memories to me. In the course of arguments about the 'Jewish question' in student clubs in Berlin in 1933, how many times did I not hear National-Socialist speakers inviting their Jewish interlocutors to disown their 'co-religionists' recently arrived from Poland, or at least to keep their distance from them. It was proper to make a distinction, they said in their smooth-tongued way; the Jews who had been Germans for generations would be treated in one way, these Polacks, weighed down by all the sins both of the Poles and of the Jews, would be treated in another.

Whom does he take me for? I shall not be guilty of such cowardice. As a sociologist I obviously do not reject distinctions inscribed on the consciousness of men and groups by centuries of history. I feel less remote from an anti-semitic Frenchman than I do from a Jew from Southern Morocco who speaks only Arabic and who has only just emerged from what seems to me like the Middle Ages or rather the impenetrable darkness of a radically alien culture. But the day a Sovereign decrees that the scattered Jews form 'a self-assured and domineering' people then I no longer have any choice. Only children defend themselves by accusing someone else: 'it wasn't me, it was him'.

Let us get back to June, 1967. I have just written of 'the almost complete unanimity' of the Jewish community. Now, this community does not exist as such, it has no organization, and neither can nor ought to have any organization. I do not know what percentage of those designated as Jews by the Vichy government are practising or non-practising or continue to belong to that 'domineering people'. But none of the Jews I know regards himself as being represented by the Consistory or by the Fonds Social Juif Unifié. The first is a civil body connected with religious observance of the Church, the second a welfare body. Neither constitutes the equivalent of a pressure group. The magazine *L'Arche* does not reflect the feelings of French Jews as a whole; for reasons that are perhaps regrettable but understandable, its editors belong to that minority of Jewish Frenchmen who are passionately attached to Israel, either out of religious conviction, or because they are Zionists, or because they are faithful to specific traditions in which no distinction is made between nation, culture and religion.

For the most part the Jews of France have never even heard of *L'Arche*. They hold the most varied opinions on every subject, some are right-wing, others left-wing. Many had revered General de Gaulle; amongst the left-wing intellectuals who were of Jewish origin there were a number of anti-Gaullists, but their attitude was much more like that of other left-wing intellectuals than that of other Jews. In short, the opinions of Jewish

Frenchmen were divided amongst the different parties more or less like those of other Frenchmen, with the proviso perhaps that the Jews preserve a sort of instinctive fidelity towards the ideas of 1789 and to the parties that invoke them, because it is to them that they owe their 'liberation'. It will be readily allowed perhaps that it is not incumbent on a Jew to support the Action Française in order to prove himself a good citizen. Moreover, a number of Jews still have ambiguous feelings about Marshal Pétain and the Vichy government. While before that German Jews had hoped for a form of National Socialism without the anti-semitism.

What is the point of recalling these well-known facts? We are now back in an age when what goes without saying goes better still if it is said. For there is something that needs to be understood: the impression given to public opinion in France that all of a sudden French Jews, scattered as they were throughout the country, formed a single block. A false impression? False in part, certainly. *Le Monde* published letters in which Jews expressed sentiments hostile to Israel and denounced her military aggression. The pacifists among the Jews did not cease being pacifists when Israel took up arms. In the special number of *Les Temps Modernes* devoted to the Israel-Arab conflict the best article supporting the Arab cause was written by a Jew, whose loneliness I respect (the Jews disowned him, the Arabs would not adopt him and the French, both pro-Israeli and anti-Israeli, looked on him with suspicion – was he Christ or Judas?).

Having said this, the fact remains that for the first time the Jews of France gave the impression of forming a sort of community. Of course, many of them protested against Edmond de Rothschild's letter, which brought back for them the old practice of the tax paid by Jews everywhere in order to succour their brethren in danger in some distant and unknown land. Left-wing intellectuals felt uncomfortable in the company of the barons of international finance. The role played by the Rothschilds, or rich people in general, in Jewish organizations has its roots in the distant past. Would the Jews who denounce or deplore this role agree to give up their time to the Consistory (when they have lost their faith) or to the Fonds National Juif Unifié (to which they send their contributions out of human respect)?

Whether they are bourgeois or intellectuals, most French

Jews these days are Jewish Frenchmen. When times are quiet they are not much concerned about their 'Jewishness', of which they are not even aware and which they only assume vis-à-vis other people out of dignity. They get annoyed or indignant when the Israelis reproach them for deserting Judaism or agreeing to assimilation. But why should they owe their fidelity to a religion when they have lost their faith, or to traditions partly imposed on them by the world around them? As I know only too well, the dialogue between assimilated (or 'de-judaized') Jews and those Jews still wedded in various ways to the way of life of their forefathers, is often lacking in friendliness.

Why, apparently, were these incompatible choices, which set Jew against Jew, reconciled with the help of a collective emotion? The answer to this question is itself going to oppose one Jew to another, I am under no illusions about that. Those of my 'co-religionists' who have remained authentically Jewish will interpret my rallying to the cause in accordance with the norms of their own mental universe. So far as they are concerned my 'Jewishness', long repressed by my determination to be thoroughly French, suddenly exploded one day and breached the dam of my reasoning faculty. I do not claim to know the final motives for my attitudes any better than anyone else. I leave everyone, Zionists and anti-semites alike, free to interpret my remarks as they like. For myself, I hold by what my own inner experience has revealed to me.

I have never been a Zionist, firstly and above all because I do not feel myself to be a Jew. It seemed to me probable that the State of Israel, simply because it existed, would lead to a prolonged conflict. I cannot agree now any more than in the past to uphold *unconditionally* the policy of the handful of men, no better and no worse than those who govern anywhere else in the world, responsible for the Israeli State. But I also know, more clearly than in the past, that in the event of the State of Israel being destroyed (an event that would be accompanied by the massacre of part of the population) I should be wounded in the very depths of my being. In this sense, I have confessed that a Jew can never achieve a perfect objectivity where Israel is concerned (the position adopted by M. Maxime Rodinson is likewise marked by its non-objectivity).

2*

The left-wing intellectuals have had the same experience, and it was more harrowing for them than for myself. Zionism in practice meant colonialism, Israel was an outpost of imperialism: these formulae, which the Communists both use and abuse, were self-evident to minds enclosed within a certain mental system. The philosophy of history which the progressives implicitly hold, places Syria on the right side and Israel, which owes its standard of living to American subsidies, on the wrong side of the barricade. The rulers of Damascus use the same language as the Paris intelligentsia, they slang the Vietnam War, President Johnson, capitalism. The rulers of Jerusalem and Tel Aviv give their citizens more bread and freedom, and forbid themselves the luxury of ideological discourse. Deep down, they may condemn the Vietnam war (though this is not certain), but they do not shout or even whisper about it.

I will go further. If an 'imperialist camp' exists, a group of countries tied closely together and obeying the same inspiration if not the same orders, how can it be denied that Israel forms part of it? The security of the Jewish State depends on the American Sixth Fleet; not that this fleet fought the Arabs but, merely by being there, it neutralized the Russian forces, restricted the theatre of operations and allowed the single combat to take place in which the Jewish soldiers won the day. Does the Israeli victory place one more success to the credit of 'American imperialism'? Yes and no. President Johnson did not know how to honour the commitment entered into by his predecessor, he was delighted that Israel should not need him in order to re-open the Gulf of Aqaba to shipping. The crisis gave him the opportunity to test the Russo-American entente, implicitly designed for the settlement of crises liable to imperil the peace of the world. He neither ordered nor provided for the start of hostilities. As for the balance sheet, there is more than one party involved. The Soviet Union now occupies in the Eastern Mediterranean more solid positions than ever before, and possesses bases on which Tsarist governments were already casting envious eyes. The Soviet fleet, still inferior to the American Sixth Fleet, is being progressively reinforced.

There is no point in denying that in the poker game of world diplomacy Israel, whether she likes it or not, is an American card; in no way a satellite of the United States but pledged for the time being to being defended by the Americans and attacked by the Russians. And the rulers of the Arab countries hate Israel all the more because they talk a more progressive language. For the rulers of Jerusalem, either in spite or because of the revolutionary socialist tradition of their first leaders, are like democrats, the social-democrats of Europe, at least in so far as the management of their economic affairs and the style of their party debates is concerned. A European statesman can at once find a common language with them, whereas he very often has great difficulty in understanding the Arab Heads of State and in sorting out what is rhetoric in their statements and what fact, what illusory and what realistic.

And finally no one, unless he be blind or fanatical, could come out wholly on one side or the other by invoking universal principles or opposing good to evil, as the intellectuals of the left love to do. As General Harkabi himself wrote in one of the articles in the special number of *Les Temps Modernes*, the Jews could not have fulfilled their national aspirations without the Arabs suffering an injustice. Both sides therefore have a cut and dried case, well supplied with impeccable arguments. For the Arabs, the very existence of Israel constitutes an act of aggression, an iniquity, a humiliation, as it did on the very first day. The Israelis have fructified the soil, welcomed the Jewish minorities driven out of Arab countries, built a State, struggled against nature, and translated into a secular reality the promises of a religion in which many of them no longer believed but to which they all remained mysteriously attached. It was a tragic confrontation, and yet no one could resign himself to the role merely of a spectator.

But is this not always the case? Which battles in the jungle where the cold-blooded monsters prowl do not deserve the epithet 'doubtful'? An Israeli student questioned me recently about a passage in Simone de Beauvoir's memoirs where she apparently says that I justified the behaviour of the British authorities over the *Exodus*. I too have some memory of that conversation. One day at the Café de Flore, Sartre and Simone de Beauvoir were loosing off their righteous wrath against the British. I pointed out that the latter had no easy task between the

Jews and the Arabs, they had not created the Israeli-Arab conflict, they were trying to arbitrate in it. At that time, Simone de
Beauvoir and Sartre were always looking for some simple divid-
ing line between angels and devils, and could see nothing except
the cruelty (or imperialism) of the British and the sacred cause of
the martyrs. I could see – and who, mindful of the future, would
not have seen it? – the struggle between Israel and the Arabs that
would follow the departure of the British, who had been unable
to impose peace or to reconcile perfectly legitimate but incompatible claims.

Those left-wing intellectuals who are of Jewish origin have
not, as J.-M. Domenach has written somewhat uncharitably,
abandoned the ground of universalism for Israeli nationalism.
They have gone through what Camus went through. There are
circumstances in which it is no good the intellectual trying to
come to some position simply by thinking, by weighing up the
pros and cons, by comparing the cases of the two sides, or by
referring himself to the abstract rules of justice. Either he says
nothing or he obeys his demon. This is what the intellectuals of
the left, both Jews and non-Jews, did in June 1967, ready to
return immediately afterwards to their normal routine.

Were Jews converted to the defence of Israel in greater
numbers and with greater passion than non-Jews? Certainly.
Does this make them 'suspect' once more? Possibly.

Let us try to state the problem in rational terms, if, things
being what they are, reason has any chance of being heard. I
would not dream of denying the fact that most Jews, even those
formerly hostile to Zionism, feel a particular sympathy for Israel,
and I would be sorry if it were otherwise. What degree of
sympathy are we allowed to have before the charge of a double
allegiance is raised? That is what I ask my fellow-countrymen,
and that is what I would even ask General de Gaulle if he were
still open to a dialogue.

From a letter in the *Nouveau Candide* written by someone 'un-
reservedly a Frenchman and, on the confessional plane, unasha-
medly an Israelite', I shall extract these historical reminders:
'Under the Restoration, French liberals, among them Armand
Carrel, a former Saint-Cyr cadet, fought against the French
Army in Spain in the ranks of the Junta. During the Greek War

of Independence Colonel Favier and several of his companions from the Empire fought alongside the Greek insurgents. During the Polish uprisings of 1830 and 1864 public opinion was pro-Polish, in spite of the government's neutrality . . . Under the Second Empire, French Catholics served and fought in the Papal army. At the beginning of the Third Republic French Catholics fought, both in Parliament and in the country, for the temporal power of the Popes . . . They were not reproached for being first and foremost Catholics . . . During the Spanish Civil War several hundred Frenchmen fought in the Nationalist and Republican ranks . . . If, tomorrow, the Vietnamese Liberation Front accepted foreign volunteers, there would be Frenchmen among them . . .'

I can already hear the objection: 'It's not the same thing'. Agreed, no two cases are ever identical, the case of the Jewish 'people' is unlike any other. I am quite ready to employ this concept of the Jewish people since on this point the Zionists are in agreement with General de Gaulle. But the concept of a 'people' acquires a peculiar significance when it is applied to the Jews; the Jews of the diaspora are not descended from the ones who lived in Palestine in Biblical times, they constitute a quasi-people because of their religious tradition and the destiny imposed on them over the centuries. The Jew who has ceased to believe or to practise is not bound to allow even the notion of a 'Jewish people'.

Why do you accept it? someone will say who is a Frenchman like myself but who has been listening to these Talmudic ratiocinations with irony. Truth to tell, I do not myself know with any certainty. However long I go on reasoning I can find no decisive motive for reproaching the Jewish Frenchman for his radical detachment in respect of his 'co-religionists', since he is no longer a believer, or of the Israelis since he wishes to be exclusively French, Gaullist or Communist. *On one condition:* that he does not push his concern for intellectual comfort to the pitch of denying the evidence. In the eyes of other people he too belongs to 'this élite people, self-assured and domineering'.

I cannot rise to such detachment nor do I want to, despite what I have written in other times. Once again, I do not refuse others the right to interpret my motives differently from myself. I am an unbeliever of the Spinoza sort, which devout Jews like least, and closer in my religious feelings to a Christian or a Buddhist than to one of my 'co-religionists', and I ought perhaps, if I carried my own logic through, to remain outside these quarrels which begin in verbal hairsplitting and often finish in blood; I refuse to pursue my own logic. As a French citizen I claim the right granted to all citizens of combining allegiance to the State with freedom of belief and of sympathy. For Jews who are believers Israel has a quite different significance than for me, but I should despise myself if I left them as the sole defenders of a freedom which I could do without more easily than they could.

'You are handing arguments to your opponents. If you, who never go to the synagogue and feel the same in front of the Wailing Wall as you do in front of the Church of the Holy Sepulchre, react with this barely-controlled passion, how are you going to prevent the anti-semites from drawing the conclusion that a Jew always remains a Jew first and foremost and a Frenchman only secondly?' Maybe I am, indeed, offering arguments to the anti-semites. Who knows? In certain circumstances everything one does is wrong. May I be forgiven, but this objection leaves me cold. Someone else will allege, equally plausibly, that silence would be taken as cowardice and that a first surrender leads to all the others. For me there is only one question: are the Jews of France, first the believers and then the rest, going to be branded as criminals because of the sympathy which most of them felt towards the State of Israel? Are they going to be required, as certain interpreters of the Presidential mind have suggested, to make not only the choice they have made already but a *total* choice? No State accepts a double allegiance (although the laws of France have allowed a number of Jews to become Israelis without losing their French nationality), but only a totalitarian State imposes an allegiance that excludes all other attachments. The Jews in the Soviet Union have known for years past, and Polish Jews found out in June, 1967, that they will never be accepted as such by a theocracy or an ideocracy.

The Fifth Republic will never become either theocratic or ideocratic but France, whether Gallican or Jacobin, is eliminating, whether deliberately or not, religious dissidence and particularities of language and culture. Bretons no longer learn

Celtic at school any more than the Basques learn their mother tongue. French education is 'de-judaizing' Jews with impressive efficiency. But it has not reduced the diversity of political convictions, a diversity which, from the historical point of view, appears to be the answer to constantly renewed and always futile attempts at spiritual unity. I know hardly any Jews who are unconditionally loyal to the State of Israel as the Communists are (or have been) to the Soviet Union. Their sympathy for a small and threatened State does not endanger the security of France. It does not stop the French government signing contracts with Iraq in order to do down the Anglo-Saxon oil companies (a trick quite in keeping with the rules of the game). It would not even have been enough to relaunch an ever-latent anti-semitism if General de Gaulle, in half a dozen highly resonant words, had not solemnly rehabilitated it.

Why did he do it? So that he could have the pleasure of shocking people? To punish the Israelis for their disobedience and the Jews for their occasional anti-Gaullism? In order solemnly to forbid any leanings towards a double allegiance? In order to sell a few more Mirages to the Arab countries? Was he aiming at the United States when he struck at the Jews? Was he trying to subject the unconditional loyalty of some of his followers, who have suffered under Charles de Gaulle, to a new test? Was he acting as the descendant of Louis xiv who would not tolerate the Protestants? Or as the heir of the Jacobins who were so fond of freedom that they forbade the citizens to have any other sentiment? I don't know. I simply know that any nationalism, carried beyond a certain point, finally corners certain Jews (of whom I am not one but whom I refuse to desert) into choosing either rejection or repudiation.

Is Gaullist nationalism going one day soon to cross this threshold? Does the Press Conference represent a watered-down version of the purge effected by Mr Gomulka in Poland in order to punish certain hesitancies?

*   *   *

The events of June, 1967 are being absorbed by the past; the Six Day War belongs to history. The Arabs, by the very excess of their misfortune and humiliation, now demand our pity. This long dissertation, which will not give complete satisfaction to anyone, is not intended to rekindle the passions of the Spring. I would like, like any man of feeling, to help bring about peace. I loathe the idea of an Israeli protectorate in Transjordania; I ask myself, like many Israelis, about the wisdom of the policy followed by the government in Jerusalem since June 12, 1967. But for as long as the war continues I do not feel I have the right to decide anything, as the Egyptian President has also declared. Now, in the final analysis, the Israelis have learnt the bitter lesson from the recent crisis that they could not, when danger threatened, rely on anyone but themselves.

The fact that the French have gone over to the Arab camp, the encouragement given by General de Gaulle to the Syrian extremists, the indifference, if not the sympathy, of French diplomacy towards the Soviet presence in the Eastern and, tomorrow, the Western Mediterranean, favour neither the preservation of a balance of power nor a progressive pacification of the area. In accordance with its apparent logic of the hour, French policy prefers a Russian hegemony to an American one; or at least it is counting on Russian might to reduce American influence. This game, which may involve certain material advantages for France, postpones any prospect of a settlement. It binds Israel even more tightly to the United States, who have been invited to supply the modern aeroplanes bought in France and paid for but whose delivery has been banned by General de Gaulle.

There is nothing and no one to stop the President of the Republic committing himself ever further along this path. The Communists, because of their anti-imperialism, and the Gaullists because of their nationalism and their hostility to Israel, will make common cause. The circle of suspicion will close once more round those men held to be responsible for the reluctance of public opinion.

I do not know whether this is a bad dream or what the immediate future actually holds. Perhaps other words will wipe away these fatal ones. Perhaps these fatal words will take on a definite and imperative meaning. This is not the moment to be afraid or hopeful, but the moment to have things out with each other, without either arrogance or false humility. In circumstances like these, the Jews, like all heterogeneous minorities bound together only by pressure from outside, are inclined to quarrel with one another. All that I ask is that they should accept the inevitable diversity of their emotional reactions and together demand the rights of free citizens in a free country.

One final word: some people have suggested that this or that motion or protest against the Press Conference was inspired by anti-Gaullism, as if René Cassin or François Jacob could be suspected of anti-Gaullism. Whoever imputes such pettiness to others must himself have a petty soul. General de Gaulle has his place in French history and every Frenchman, whether he be a Gaullist or not, Jew or non-Jew, must passionately hope that for the man of the Eighteenth of June old age will not be a shipwreck.

How many Jews, in France and outside France, wept after the Press Conference not because they were afraid of persecution but because they had lost their hero! How many still hope to recover what they have lost!

What has been said can no longer be unsaid, but tomorrow's comment or silence will decide the final meaning of a few words which will, in part, define the last phase of Gaullism.

December 28, 1967.

Part 2
During the Crisis

Part 2
During the Crisis

Sound of Arms in
the Near East[1]

The withdrawal of the Peacekeeping Force at the very moment
when the danger is mounting in the Near East has its value as a
symbol. The soldiers of the United Nations can keep the combatants apart for just as long as they want to be kept apart. They
are incapable of imposing peace because they do not have the
material means of doing so, and they do not have these means
because all States, both big and small, pursue their own self-
interest. Often in agreement when it comes to stopping conflict
spreading, they are almost never in agreement when it comes to
resolving problems.

For the time being the problems remain insoluble, whether it
be that of the rivalry between conservatives and revolutionaries
in the Arab States or that of the coexistence of these States with
Israel. Peace cannot be established by diplomatic procedures,
but this still does not imply that military operations are either
imminent or inevitable.

In spite of the disquiet which the sound of arms awakes in the
Chancellories, the specialists remain relatively optimistic, in so far
as they assume that events will not escape from the control of the
leading actors. How could Nasser contemplate a new Sinai campaign, when a significant proportion of his troops are involved
in the Yemen? Syria cannot take on the Israeli army if it only has
its own forces to call on. Syria's rulers, although many observers
hold them to be irresponsible, know very well that Egypt is
today in a position of weakness and must await more favourable
circumstances before a new trial of strength with Israel. Israel
is still Nasser's absolute and permanent enemy, but, in the short

[1] Written on May 21 and published in the *Figaro* of May 23, before President
Nasser had announced the closing of the Gulf of Aqaba.

term, his true adversaries are the royalists in the Yemen and the moderates in Aden and South Arabia, who must be eliminated or overthrown in order to open up the way to his distant goal.

The most plausible and commonly accepted interpretation of the present crisis is based on this analysis, and on the intentions, known or assumed, of the statesmen involved. Since neither the government in Jerusalem nor that in Cairo wants war, then, logically, no war should take place. And why should Soviet diplomacy, whatever objectives are imputed to it, seek to provoke military operations which would not work out to the benefit of its protégés?

This prognosis of the situation as a whole remains the most plausible. Unfortunately other, less predictable elements must also be taken into consideration. For a number of years now the Israeli government has been following a policy of 'limited reprisals'. Whenever there is an attack or sabotage by Arab guerrilla bands, units of the regular army inflict 'punishment' on the country held to be responsible. The recent reprisal raid on a Jordanian village was a subject of bitter debate in Israel itself, where everyone knows that King Hussein is hostile to the terrorist activity encouraged by the government in Damascus, although the infiltrations are carried out across the border between Jordan and Israel.

The source of the immediate danger is the twin threat of the Arab guerrillas and Israeli reprisals, for it is yet to be proved that any government, either in Damascus or Cairo, would be in a position, even if it were firmly decided to, to bring to a complete halt the activities of the guerrillas. President Nasser's recent decisions have two obvious objectives: to dissuade Israel from carrying out its doctrine of reprisals in the future, and to force the conservative governments in Arabia to display their solidarity with the revolutionary governments, Israel being, in terms of both ideologies, the one true enemy.

The departure of the Peacekeeping Force means that we must take into account another, even more serious eventuality. Since the Sinai campaign of 1956 the port of Eilat has been open to shipping. This opening represents the main advantage derived by Israel from her military successes. Over the past eleven years, a United Nations' contingent, stationed at the strategic point, has as it were symbolized Egypt's assent to freedom of movement in the Gulf of Aqaba. The return of Egyptian soldiers still does not signify any change in Cairo's policy, but it at least signifies the threat of a change.

Agreed, the Israeli government has let it be known that such a change would constitute a *casus belli*. But even then, the exchange of threat and counter-threat, of dissuasion and counter-dissuasion, hardly enables us to predict the outcome. For the side that is the stronger locally will not necessarily dissuade the other; a lot depends also on the support which they each expect to receive from the Great Powers. Now, in recent months, Russian diplomacy has shown itself to be increasingly active in the whole region between Casablanca and the Red Sea, both in word and in deed.

In word, it has upheld the Syrian and revolutionary cause against Western imperialism and its 'accomplices in Israel'. Those Arab countries held to be 'progressive', Syria as well as Algeria, have received really quite considerable quantities of arms. Tunisia and Morocco have become increasingly afraid of an 'arms race', of which it will be North Africa's turn, after the Near East, to be the scene.

Here again, it would be wrong to conclude that the object of Moscow's policy was to start hostilities whose victims would be those Arab countries of a non-revolutionary disposition. For the present, this policy is restricted to reinforcing those States which seem to it most hostile towards the United States and Great Britain, while also displaying, in many different ways, its presence in the Mediterranean. The Soviet navy now has bases there, where it is genuinely welcome. This Russian presence adds to the complexity of the situation: we do not know, indeed, to what extent Moscow would tolerate Israeli reprisals or military success in 1967 as it did in 1956. Now, the decisions that will be taken in Damascus or in Cairo depend to a great extent on the plans and intentions attributed by the Syrians and Egyptians to the leaders in Moscow.

Thus, once we have admitted that it is in no one's interest to provoke a major crisis in the present state of things, there are still two main reasons why uncertainty remains: the Arab governments are not fully in control of the activities of the terrorist units; the dialectic of mutual intimidation would seem less unpredictable if the rivalry of the Great Powers did not threaten to overthrow the logic of the local balance of strength.

Russia versus America[1]

Nothing could better illustrate the suddenness of the Near Eastern crisis than to recall the remarks made in Cairo, on May 12 last, by M. Hervé Alphand, the secretary-general of the Foreign Ministry: 'France and the UAR are neighbours in that they both take the same view of the independence of nations and of non-interference in the internal affairs of other States and in their disinterested cooperation.'[2]

Only a week ago, the secretary-general of the Israeli Foreign Ministry was getting ready to set off on his travels oblivious of the coming storm. The conclusion is inescapable: the present crisis was brought about deliberately and not by accident. The moment was probably chosen in advance. It was President Nasser who took the decision but, behind him, it is hard not to suppose that Moscow had agreed. The deliveries of Soviet arms to the Arab countries, which had been speeded up in recent months and which General Béthouart had commented on in this newspaper, heralded the storm that had indeed been feared by British observers. I had heard about it at length from my friends in London last month.

We can only speculate about the intentions of Russian diplomacy, but it is tempting to relate the events in the Near East to those in South-East Asia. The rulers of the Soviet Union, for whom it is materially impossible to intervene actively in Vietnam, in all probability consider that, by going on bombing North Vietnam, the Americans are violating the unwritten rules of 'peaceful coexistence'. Having been forced to tolerate 'American aggression' against a Communist state, with no other means of replying to it than by supplying arms, the men in the Kremlin

[1] Written on May 25 and printed in the *Figaro* on the 26th, when President Nasser's decision to close the Gulf of Aqaba had become known.
[2] M. Alphand has told me that his remarks were inaccurately reported.

consider it their right to display their strength and influence in a
more favourable theatre of operations. The Mediterranean is not
an American lake and the Arab countries most hostile to the
West may not be Communist, but they do share common
interests with the Soviet Union.

At the same time one can see the limits of what one was ready
to call the rapprochement between Russia and America. Perhaps
this rapprochement would have been strengthened but for the
war in Vietnam. For the present, it does not go beyond a firm
resolve not to be involved in a major war. In this respect the
American analysts have been good teachers, they have success-
fully convinced the Soviet leaders that to resort to nuclear
weapons would be a catastrophe for everyone, and thus a madness. But this lesson, though it may stave off the worst, has its
own dangers. The less afraid Heads of State are of a major war, the
readier they are to resign themselves to waging minor ones. The
new fact may well be precisely this sort of security. Since nuclear
war is 'impossible' the other forms of war become possible once
again. The dialectic worked out theoretically – that stability at
the nuclear level implies increased instability at the level of
traditional weapons – is unfortunately being confirmed, as it
were, experimentally.

No one can say, for the present, just how far President Nasser
and the Russian leaders are prepared to go. It can hardly be
doubted that Nasser has had assurances from the Russians, but
the Egyptian President may have placed an interpretation on
Mr Gromyko's remarks which the latter himself would not have
accepted. Moreover, the moment the Great Powers promise help
to small ones and stake their prestige, they cease to be entirely
in control of events. The so-called supporting actors, whether in
Hanoi or Cairo, may well involve the so-called protagonists in
adventures of this sort.

In such circumstances, any commentary risks being overtaken
by events before it has even appeared. This morning, May 25,
a diplomatic poker game is going on. Israel will not accept the
closing of the Gulf of Aqaba, and, on this point, the United States
and Great Britain support the government in Jerusalem un-
reservedly. General de Gaulle has not committed himself, but
is apparently saving himself for the task of mediation.

But one would need to be mighty optimistic to believe that negotiations between ambassadors or ministers will enable a way out to be found. President Nasser is not going to go back on mining the Gulf of Aqaba unless he gets compensation. Unless he is offered something Moscow has no reason for bringing pressure to bear on him. In short, either a military confrontation between Israel and the Arab countries or a strategic and diplomatic confrontation between the Soviet Union and the United States seems necessary for any settlement. The first has already taken shape on the ground, where the armies have been mobilized and stand facing one another, the second has not as yet passed the verbal stage.

Until 1914, diplomats would almost have despaired of a peaceful solution. In the past twenty years they have grown used to living dangerously, to looking on crises as substitutes for wars and to trusting in the (relative) wisdom of the two Great Powers.

In spite of everything, the reasons for this ambiguous optimism are still with us.

The Hour of Decision[1]

President Nasser has ensured himself the advantage of the first move. By causing the Peacekeeping Force to be withdrawn and closing the Gulf of Aqaba, he has thrown down a challenge both to the United States, which had solemnly pledged itself not to stand for a blockade of Eilat, and to Israel, which had declared that such a blockade would constitute a *casus belli*. He has thrown the eventual responsibility for hostilities on to the enemy, on to Israel and her protectors. Having seized possession of the stakes, he has forced others into militarily offensive actions, although, politically speaking, these would simply be a rejoinder. If the aggressor is the man who fires the first shot then the Egyptian operation, abetted by the glaring inexperience of the Secretary-General of the United Nations, has condemned Israel to the role of aggressor. The way the drama develops after this first act depends above all on two actors and two only, the United States and Israel.

In fact, the rulers of all the Arab States, whatever their feelings may be privately, have been obliged to make common cause against the absolute enemy, the one whose right to exist is denied, Israel. It will be only at a later stage that the possible dissension between the two Arab camps, the traditional and the progressive, can show itself.

France, which has ceased to be Israel's ally since the end of the Algerian war, has resolved energetically not to take sides, while concealing her inability to act by putting forward a plan for 'concerted action' by the four 'Great Powers'. This habitual formula, which chimes with General de Gaulle's favourite philosophy, is indeed blameless, with the single reservation that it presupposes a world with nothing in common with today's world, the world

---

[1] Written on May 28, published in the *Figaro* on the 29th.

as it was before 1914 in which the great powers, without thereby putting an end to their rivalry, sometimes managed to agree among themselves in order to impose a peaceful settlement in some secondary conflict.

There is no concert of the world as there was once a concert of Europe. The Soviet Union and the United States have certain interests in common, though hardly in the Near East, apart obviously from their shared concern not to be drawn into hazardous enterprises by the passions of one side or the other. One would have had to be very naïve or ignorant to have thought that the Soviet Union, after sending, in past months, hundreds of tanks to the Near East, would bring pressure to bear on President Nasser in the direction hoped for by Washington. Needless to say, General de Gaulle was under no illusions, but, having opted for neutrality, he lets events follow their own course. Diplomacy is either action or a cover-up for inaction, as the case may be.

The United States and, subsidiarily, Great Britain seem to have hovered between two policies. Naturally, both the Americans and the British remembered their commitment in respect of Israel and the principle of freedom of movement in the Gulf of Aqaba. In such circumstances words mean nothing or, to be more precise, they can take on two radically opposed meanings. They herald either the decision to resort to force or else the provisional acceptance of the *fait accompli*, with the vague promise of extracting by negotiation what one has forborne to conquer by arms. Speaking on behalf of France in 1936, M. Albert Sarraut would not stand for Strasbourg 'remaining beneath the mouths of German cannon' – which meant that French troops would not be going into the Rhineland. President Johnson's first statement was ambiguous in just the same way. The crisis would have been defused if three thousand British and American marines had been landed at Sharm-el-Sheik as a temporary replacement for the UN force. The American mixture of firm speaking and passivity shed the major responsibility on to Israel.

At no time since 1948 have the rulers of Israel found themselves in so tragic a predicament, never have they had to take a decision so heavy with consequences, so laden with 'sweat,

blood and tears'. They cannot keep their army – which forms
ten per cent of the total population – under arms for weeks on
end, or even for many days. Now, what the Soviet Union, Egypt
and France are asking is that Israel should resign itself to the
temporary closing of the Gulf of Aqaba and consent to diplomatic procedures.

But why should President Nasser make concessions after a
diplomatic success? Why should Mr Kosygin help Mr Johnson
to keep his promises? In any case, Russian diplomacy has been
marking up points by fomenting hostility towards the United
States. If the latter, Israel's protectors, appear at the same time
unable to protect her, the profits will be twofold.

*   *   *

And so the handful of men responsible for the two and a half
million Jews who have built the State of Israel are face to face
with their destiny and their consciences. They are on their own.
The threat of extermination has again been sounded by the voice
of President Nasser. What is at stake is no longer the Gulf of
Aqaba, but the existence of the State of Israel, that State which
all the Arab countries see as a foreign body that must sooner or
later be eliminated and whose citizens have sworn to defend it
with their lives. To launch military operations today against the
coalition of Arab States would not be a repetition of the Sinai
campaign. The Egyptian bombers would not be destroyed on
the ground by French and British planes. Medium-range ballistic
missiles supplied to the Egyptians by the Russians might strike
at Jerusalem and Tel Aviv right from the start of the war. Even
a successful encounter would solve nothing, but simply afford a
breathing-space like that of the past eleven years. And in the
opposite event, a surrender would open the way for another
confrontation in the near future in circumstances that might be
even more unfavourable.

Everyone who knows the Israeli leaders must have a presenti-
ment of the probable outcome of their deliberations.

Face to Face with Tragedy

This article, written on June 4 and published in the *Figaro Littéraire* for June 12, was preceded by a note written on June 8:

I wrote the following article on the morning of June 4, unable to choose between the language of confession and that of analysis. As I write this postscript it has been 'outdated' and will have been further so by the time it appears: the hostilities will be over, and the Israeli troops, the field theirs, will have let the diplomats take over.

It is too late to write another article, too soon to draw the lesson from the events. Since my friends at the *Figaro Littéraire* consider that this meditation by a Jewish Frenchman has a significance beyond the circumstances that gave rise to it, I have left it as it was written, in anguish and also in the awareness of contradictions which it is not up to me to overcome.

One last word. Israel might have been beaten and her defeat would have been total. If, as their propaganda had boasted, Syrians, Jordanians and Egyptians had met up in Tel Aviv, the State of Israel would not have survived, even if Israeli lives had been saved. Israel has not defeated the Arab States; by a lightning operation it has won a military success which will not be decisive politically. The vice that had been closing on this small country has been broken, President Nasser has lost face, the Egyptians do not yet know how to use the tanks and modern aircraft with which the Soviet Union had been supplying them.

More than ever today we must keep a cool head. The one objective is not victory but peace. Israel will only live in peace the day she is accepted by the Arabs who, tomorrow as today, will still be her neighbours, more numerous than the Israelis and, in the more or less distant future, will themselves become technologically proficient. Let us adjure the great powers to use this breathing-space to seek, at last, the means of bringing peace to a part of the world where, for the past twenty years, there has existed only a belligerent armistice.

I am haunted by a memory: after the first world war, Paul Desjardins wrote a preface which ended with the words: 'And so it will have been necessary that these children and our own children died so that we should know that they would have understood one another'.

How long must it be before Jews and Muslims, Israelis and Arabs, who believe in the same God, manage to understand one another?

*   *   *

No Jew, whether a believer or an unbeliever, Zionist or anti-Zionist, can be objective when what is at stake is Israel and the two and a half million Jews who built a State in a land equally Holy for the faithful of the three great religions of the Book.

I am what is known as an 'assimilated Jew'. As a child I wept over France's disasters at Waterloo or Sedan, but not as I listened to the account of the destruction of the Temple. The only flag and the only national anthem that will bring tears to my eyes are the tricolour and the *Marseillaise*. It was Hitler, almost forty years ago now, who revealed my 'Jewishness' to me. Come what may I have striven to assume it, which simply means never to conceal it. As I see it, there is neither dishonour nor glory in being a Jew, I am neither ashamed nor proud or it; nor do I have the right to put humanity in the dock, or at least no more so than any man of feeling, just because I survived the Final Solution.

Since Hitler, I have always known that France's interests would not always or necessarily coincide with those of the Jews or the Israelis. As a French citizen, I felt myself spontaneously responsible for an infinitesimal share, one forty-five millionth, of the destiny of France. Having been born into a Jewish family I owed it to myself not to deny my membership of a distant and, for a long time, almost abstract community, my community, for as long as men's cruelty and passions should expose it to persecution.

I lived in Germany between 1931 and 1933, and I had few

illusions about the fate in store for France, but I hesitated to speak out. Only too often, friends regarded me with barely disguised suspicion when I told them the future that awaited them as well as myself. And so I said nothing. Moreover, a thesis on the philosophy of history was taking up all my time: since Hitler was going to make war I needed to finish it as soon as possible (I had my viva in March 1938, two days after the German troops went into Austria).

After the war the situation was reversed. Since it ended, I have been able to write in support of a reconciliation with Germany without being suspect, at a time when indignation, so reticent when it might have done some good, was being given free rein. (What writer will decide one day to deal with the cases of Roosevelt and Churchill, who might easily have spoken out, and whose words, much more than Pius XII's, might perhaps have saved millions of lives?)

In the past twenty years, since chance brought me to the *Figaro*, I have not experienced any contradiction between my duty as a Frenchman and my moral obligations as a Jew. In practice, if not in theory, anti-semitism seemed to be the other side of the iron curtain. As I saw it, France's interests would be served by the building of a united Europe and by the Atlantic alliance. France was split by decolonization, but in that respect the Jews shared the same fate as all Frenchmen.

It was not as a Jew that I came out in favour of Algerian independence. Agreed, this independence, as it has turned out, involved its own measure of injustices and these did not spare the Jews of North Africa, who were more affected by them than anyone else. Rightly or wrongly, it seemed to me that the least injustice and the interests of France coincided. In 1956 Pierre Brisson taxed me with my hostility to the Suez expedition: I told him that I was a French citizen and that, what was more, I did not think it any more consistent with France's interests to be at war with the whole Arab world than with Israel's to be joining in the last battle of France's Empire.

The alliance between France and Israel – I greatly shocked many people by writing as much in the *Figaro Littéraire* a few years back – was not built to last a thousand years. Once Algeria was independent, General de Gaulle – and any other Head of

3

State or government leader would have done the same in his position – resumed relations with all the countries in the Near East; he tried to give France back the intellectual, moral and economic position she had occupied there. When the crisis broke a few days ago he forbore to choose between the conflicting parties. Radio and television affected to be neutral but hypocritically upheld the Egyptian case. Gaullists were disappointed, Jews indignant and Jewish Gaullists stunned. All were wrong. We have the right to judge Gaullist diplomacy as a whole as to whether it conforms or conflicts with France's true interests, but if, as a famous formula has it, France has neither friends nor enemies but only interests, what right have we to protest on this occasion?

There are hundreds of millions of Muslims throughout the world, and tens of millions of Arabs; there are only two and a half million Israelis. In any case, France has no means of acting in the Near East. By choosing atomic weapons at the expense of conventional ones, she has, in effect, chosen a diplomacy of neutrality or, if you prefer, of friendly relations with all States. This neutrality expresses itself in an anti-American language not, as is thoughtlessly said, because General de Gaulle has never forgiven the Americans for having spurned him twenty years ago, but because he can get from them for nothing everything he might ask them for. It is not up to the United States to deprive France of the American military presence in Europe, the Atlantic alliance or NATO. And so France is free to lavish smiles and encouragement on all enemies of the United States. By cutting herself adrift from her Atlantic allies, France can escape the opprobrium connected with 'American imperialism' or even 'Western imperialism'. Once again, I am not judging the ultimate merits, the cost or the benefits of this diplomacy, but, once it has been allowed, why should President de Gaulle alienate President Nasser by recommending him to open the Gulf of Aqaba?

There are two alternatives: either the United States will default on the solemn commitment entered into in 1957 towards the government in Jerusalem and will lose face; and is that going to upset General de Gaulle? Or else the United States, by a combination of diplomacy and force, will restore freedom of movement in the Gulf and achieve a sort of compromise; then

General de Gaulle will perhaps get a share of the credit. In any case, he remains a possible mediator. He can argue that he is doing more for Israel by refusing to take sides (despite the sorrow and indignation of the Israelis, who are too worked up to grasp the subtleties of the game). Once again, I abstain from judgment.

Is there any advantage for a second-rank nation in going it alone? Is it in France's interests never again to agree to co-operate with the Anglo-Saxons? To place her trust in the peaceful intentions of the Soviet Union and the friendship of the Third World? A moment of crisis in the Middle East is not one when a French Jew can reply calmly to such questions.

*   *   *

But enough of problems of conscience; let us go back to being what we normally try to be, the observer seeking to understand and to help others to understand.

In a way, the Near Eastern crisis is a permanent one. The Arab countries have never accepted the existence of the State of Israel. For the past twenty years it has lived in a state of siege. A whole people under arms; the army is the people and the people the army. Since their fathers and mothers were led to the gas-chambers with the complicity of some people and amidst the indifference of others, and since there are today people unthinking or pharisaical enough to accuse the victims of not having defended themselves, the Israelis, if they have to die, are going to die with their guns in their hands.

Why has this endemic crisis suddenly become explosive? We must be fair and distinguish known facts from plausible speculation. Known facts: President Nasser, unable to bring the war in the Yemen to an end, unable to pay the interest on loans contracted outside, unable to get food supplies from the United States to feed his population, found himself, so to speak, constrained to some dazzling coup. Several times, during the past few years, he had advised moderation on the other Heads of State; they must always be thinking of the final conflict, he had proclaimed, the one that would wipe Israel off the map, but what was the good of bringing that up until they had the superiority? Only last year I was expounding to the Israelis the reasons for a short-term optimism: why should the explosion take place while the Arab countries were divided, and the strength of the Israeli army and the weakness of the Egyptian army so apparent? I was wrong, and my listeners were also over-optimistic. In order to restore a minimum of unity amongst the Arab countries President Nasser was, so to speak, forced to play poker. The very excess of the conflicts between Arabs pushed Egypt into uniting them all against the common enemy, the absolute enemy, the one whose right to existence even was not recognized.

Other established facts: the deliveries of Soviet arms to all the Arab countries, from the Red Sea to the Maghreb. Why so many tanks in Iraq, in Egypt, even in Algeria? Many but not contradictory answers to these questions suggest themselves.

Since the Cuban crisis at the end of 1962, the détente in Europe has grown; Russian domination of the Socialist countries of Eastern Europe has relaxed, Romania has shown her independence; on the other side France has left NATO. The Soviet Union can no longer open a front of the cold war on the Old Continent, her allies would not agree to it and the probable result would be a restoration of the Atlantic alliance.

Should the Soviet Union, at all events, have opened another front and, after her failures in Cuba and in Berlin, sought the opportunity for revenge? I am not sure. In all probability the Vietnam war is one of the reasons for the threat of war which hangs over the Near East today. But in any case, two patterns of development, one military, the other diplomatic, have taken shape in recent years and have both led up to the present events.

The Soviet leaders have finally adhered to the ideas on strategy of the American leaders. They have realized that nuclear and thermonuclear weapons have only an indirect influence on the relations between nations. Of course, her capacity for a nuclear response makes the Soviet Union safe from any attack on her territory, but it does not enable her to instal ballistic missiles in Cuba or to prevent the bombing of North Vietnam. Precisely because it is hard to conceive of these monstrous weapons being used except in extreme situations, the 'old' diplomacy goes on. Diplomacy 'as usual', as the English would put it. Neither the forty-one nuclear submarines nor the hundreds of Minutemen serve as instruments essential to American action.

They ensure the necessary preconditions for that action, but it is the Sixth Fleet in the Mediterranean and the Seventh Fleet in the Far East which enable them to make war or keep the peace. The Russians have grasped this in their turn, and Mr Khrushchev's successors have strengthened the traditional armaments of their country, especially the navy. Soviet submarines and surface vessels show the flag with increasing frequency in the Far East and the Mediterranean.

*   *   *

Simultaneously, the Soviet Union, which could not compete with Mao's China in revolutionary verbiage nor at home return to the methods of a primitive Stalinism, must have been tempted by a third course, that of an expansion towards the traditional objectives of Russian ambition, especially since this third course offered them at the same time the chance of 'whipping-in' the so-called under-developed or socialist countries. From New Delhi to Havana they have all declared themselves pro-Egyptian and anti-Israeli.

That President Nasser should want openly to destroy a member State of the United Nations does not trouble the delicate conscience of Mrs Gandhi. 'State-cide', admittedly, is not genocide. And those French Jews who have given their souls to all the black, brown or yellow revolutionaries, are now screaming with pain while their friends are screaming for a death. I suffer like them and with them, whatever they may have said or done, not because we have become Zionists or Israelis, but because an irresistible feeling of solidarity is mounting in us. It matters little where it comes from. If the Great Powers, in accordance with the cold calculation of their own interests, allow the small State which is not my own to be destroyed, this crime, a modest one in terms of numbers, would deprive me of the strength to live, and I believe that millions upon millions of men would feel ashamed of the human race.

But let us resume the language of the analyst. We must hope that, for the time being, there is to be no question of what Hitler called the final solution and what the Egyptian President calls the decisive battle.

The first round has taken place and President Nasser has won it. The United States, involved in Vietnam in a war it cannot manage either to win or to lose and whose best if not only justification is the duty the Americans have to safeguard the value of their pledge to the Vietnamese, was taken unawares by the suddenness of the steps taken by both sides; U Thant gave in to Nasser's injunctions more quickly than the latter expected or perhaps even wanted. President Johnson did not have the wit to forestall the blockade of the Gulf of Aqaba by some symbolic message. The general passivity, during the four crucial days, brought over even his enemies to the apparent victor. In order to save themselves, the Arab Heads of State have joined in a venture aimed as much at them as at Israel. The latter who, only two weeks ago, was threatening to take the law into her own hands if the *fedayin* kept up their raids, now found herself surrounded by enemies temporarily united.

What is the point of wondering now whether the Soviet Union launched the operation or simply gave permission for it, or whether U Thant precipitated it by his inexperience or Johnson by his indecision at the critical hour? On June 4, 1967, the armies of Israel and the Arab countries are face to face in the desert, ready to fight it out, just as the Soviet Union and the United States are confronting one another on the diplomatic plane, determined not to destroy each other, but not to reach agreement.

How the War became Inevitable[1]

Half a century has gone by yet historians have so far failed to agree about the precise degree of responsibility of the two sides for originating the first world war. It would be presumptuous, therefore, while the din of the present battle still echoes, to pretend to the role of judge. It would be a particularly futile undertaking at a time when the archives are still closed, the participants still alive and when everyone's mind is exposed to hypotheses that are plausible but not capable of proof.

In spite of these reservations, the broad outlines of the drama stand out strongly. All one needs to do to follow them is to pick up the file of newspapers for the past few months. Before 1967, as before 1956, Soviet arms flowed into the Near East. This time they even went as far as the Maghreb. The Soviet Union is a great power and, even if we ignore the Vietnam war, is within its rights to take an interest in this part of the world which has ceased to be a game reserve of the West. What is more, any Russia, the Tsar's as much as Lenin's, will try to gain an outlet to the warm seas and to extend its influence over the coastal countries of the Eastern Mediterranean.

Before 1967 as before 1956, relations between the United Arab Republic and the United States had deteriorated. John Foster Dulles had refused to finance the building of the Aswan Dam. Recently, the American representatives laid down conditions which President Nasser would not accept for further shipments of agricultural surpluses. Once again, the United Arab Republic was at the end of its economic tether, unable to pay its debts or to finance the investments necessary for economic development. The Arab States had never been so fractious; an important part

[1] Written on June 6 and published in the *Figaro* of June 7.

of the Egyptian army was tied down in the Yemen in an interminable war against the Royalist tribesmen and, indirectly,
against Saudi Arabia.

Did the military coup in Greece and the Israeli General Rabin's
threats against Syria lead President Nasser to fear an American
plot of which he would be the next victim? Did Mr Gromyko
make him promises in March? We shall leave these questions
unanswered. In order to recover his prestige as a leader, and in
order to recreate the unity of the Arab States, President Nasser
had one weapon at his command, still the same weapon and
perhaps the only one: to act against Israel.

For eleven years he had tolerated the UN contingents in the
Gaza Strip and at Sharm-el-Sheik. The United Nations soldiers
kept the peace along the border and symbolized the freedom of
all ships to use the Gulf of Aqaba. For eleven years they enabled
the Egyptian President to tolerate the suspension of terrorism
and the opening up of Eilat, the one lasting advantage Israel
derived from her victory in Sinai.

It was at this moment that one man took a decision which
seemed senseless then and, in retrospect, seems fatal: without
consulting either the Security Council or the General Assembly
of the United Nations, U Thant fell in with the injunctions of
President Nasser, who was perhaps not asking him to do so.

The Secretary-General of the United Nations may have been
acting in accordance with what was legal. The UN force, which
was only stationed on one side of the frontier, could not remain
on a country's territory without that country's consent. But any
man endowed with a minimum of political awareness would have
realized that more than legality it was the fate of the peace that
was at stake. U Thant should have given way in principle to
President Nasser's demand; he could then have played for time,
and mobilized world opinion against a danger glaring to everyone's eyes but his own. Even today there is nothing to prove
that President Nasser would not have accepted being 'held back'.

*   *   *

The very rapidity of this initial success incited the gambler to a
second throw of the dice. There remained one last evidence of

the 1956 defeat: the port of Eilat was open to shipping and through it Israel received her petrol and exported her products to the Far East. During the twenty-four hours following the departure of the UN troops the blockade of the Gulf of Aqaba was proclaimed in terms that still left room for interpretation. John Foster Dulles had given formal assurances to Israel in 1957, but these assurances did not commit the United Nations. For forty-eight hours destiny hesitated. It was incumbent on President Johnson to honour the commitments entered into ten years earlier by a President of the United States or, rather, he must, by the solemnity of his statements and the eloquence of his public or private messages, not leave Cairo or Moscow in any doubt as to his determination. The American President, weighed down by an interminable war in the Far East and rightly suspecting Soviet influence behind Egypt's defiance, promised diplomatic aid so hesitantly that he provoked a chain reaction on both sides which led infallibly to the explosion.

Within a few days, President Nasser had become a hero once again, the conqueror, the man who could restore their lands to the Palestinians and their honour to the Arabs. All the kings, Hussein, Faisal, whatever their private feelings may have been, allowed themselves to be swept along by the wave of enthusiasm which was unfurling. It matters little whether it was patriotism or self-interest. Yesterday's enemies had embraced and were united against a common enemy and by a sincere fervour.

The Arabs were fired by hope, the Israelis, whom everyone had deserted, by the fierce ardour of despair. They were ready to die and they would go down fighting. Nasser could no longer pull back: the hour of the decisive battle had sounded. Israel could wait no longer: the Gulf of Aqaba had been closed and Iraqi troops were entering Jordan.

President Nasser had made the war possible, U Thant and President Johnson had made it inevitable.[1]

*　　*　　*

Israel is fighting for its life, but military success will afford her only a breathing-space. Tomorrow, just as yesterday, she will be

[1] Looking back on it, this seems to me too harsh a judgment on these two men.

3*

surrounded by Arab States. The two Great Powers are incapable of agreeing about anything except not to destroy one another. Yet the only hope, in Jerusalem as in Hanoi, remains a reasoned dialogue between the Powers.

The Tragic Ironies of History[1]

Men make their history, but they do not know what history they are making; the Middle East crisis, whose second act is now finishing (the third act will be a diplomatic one), illustrates, yet once more, this banal formula. The principal actors took their decisions after weighing up the chances and the risks, but, all in all, these have led to results that do not answer to the objectives of any of them, perhaps not even to the objectives of the Israeli leaders.

So far as the development of the crisis goes, there are still phases of it that are in shadow. We do not know what Mr Gromyko said to President Nasser last March. We do not know what significance should have been given to General Rabin's threats against Syria. We do not know whether, as he asserts, the Egyptian President really did fear an Israeli attack on Syria. But, these uncertainties apart, the principal facts are not in doubt.

President Nasser was well aware, as his own statements show, that by decreeing the closing of the Gulf of Aqaba to shipping, by massing his troops in Sinai, by concluding a pact with Jordan and by inciting Iraqi units to join the Jordanian troops, he was challenging Israel. The leaders of that country had said and repeated that the blockade of Eilat or the entry of Iraqi troops into Jordan would constitute a *casus belli*. Since the Arab States did not recognize the State of Israel and since Egypt invoked a state of war in order to bar the Suez Canal to Israeli ships, international law was, so to speak, excluded from the argument.

To resort to the language of the philosophers, Israel and her neighbours were living in a state of nature, where strength and

[1] Written on June 13, published in the *Figaro* on June 14.

cunning prevail. Egypt and Israel both invoked the principle formulated by Montesquieu: 'Between societies, the right of natural defence sometimes involves the necessity of attack when one people sees that a continuance of peace would put another people in a position to destroy it and that, at that moment, attack is the only means of preventing this destruction.'

Israel, it is true, might have quoted the following lines from *L'Esprit des Lois*: 'Small societies more often have the right to make war than large ones, because they are more often in a position to be destroyed.' But, here again, everyone will take his own line: the national product of two and a half million Israelis is almost as high as that of thirty million Egyptians, the *per capita* product is almost ten times higher in Israel than in Egypt.

The nature of the battlefield ensured a huge advantage to whoever struck first. On May 26, the Soviet Union and the United States brought pressure to bear on President Nasser not to make the first move towards war. In this instance the two Great Powers acted in the way they have got used to acting in, that is, although determined to avoid a direct confrontation, they have not given up their vicarious rivalry through small powers. But one of the two Great Powers at least, the Soviet Union, was right to 'hold back' Egypt, for want of the means of supplying her with military aid should war start; they must also have asked themselves first of all whether the United States, for their part, would or could 'hold back' Israel, and what would be the outcome of the fighting in the event of Israel refusing to allow herself to be 'held back'.

Both President Johnson and President de Gaulle, each in his own manner, gave it as his explicit aim to 'hold back' Israel. But they did it in such a way as inevitably to bring about, if we take them at their word, what they were seeking to avoid. The French President forgot the commitments entered into in respect of Israel by the governments of the Fourth Republic in 1957; not even verbally did he uphold the Israeli thesis about the opening of the Gulf of Aqaba. He went much further since he unequivocally threatened to consider as the aggressor the side that fired the first shot, fully knowing that Israel risked signing her own death warrant if she accepted diplomatic defeat and left the initiative with the Arab States.

President Johnson came out in favour of the Israeli thesis over the Gulf of Aqaba, but he also made an error of calculation (assuming it was his aim to stop a war). He acted as if the promise of diplomatic action would be enough for Israel, as if the already hostile armies massed on both sides of the line of demarcation could stay facing one another for days or even weeks. Mr Harold Wilson, on the other hand, seems to have had the correct intuition: only an immediate military action in the Straits of Aqaba would have defused the bomb whose explosion has just devastated the Holy Land.

None the less, in retrospect, both President Johnson and President de Gaulle have a way of justifying themselves. The first, it will be said, knew the Israeli armed forces to be superior. By not intervening he prevented any military intervention by the Soviet Union and thus enabled Israel to win a victory which, as well as being an Israeli victory, would also be an American victory or, at least, a defeat for Russia. If this is really what went on in the American President's mind then American policy seems admirable in a Machiavellian sort of way.

As for the French President, if his true aim was, as usual, to keep his distance from what is normally called the West, and if he was anxious above all that France should not be associated with 'American imperialism' or 'Anglo-Saxon imperialism', then in spite of everything, he succeeded. Although opinion in France was massively pro-Israeli, he earned the compliments of President Nasser and the acclamation of Arab crowds. Mirages, built in France and flown by Israelis, destroyed the MIGs, built in Russia and flown by Egyptians, while, during the crisis, French policy was always much closer to the Russian line than to the American. To judge by the public opinion polls most Frenchmen were not aware of this. However, M. Pompidou is wrong when he asserts that the French government has not lost the confidence of the government in Jerusalem. Such an assertion would only hold water if it were admitted that France's action at a time of acute crisis was, in any case, of no consequence.

Among the actors in the drama there are two who have to admit that their calculations were wrong: the Soviet Union, forced on June 6 to accept an unconditional cease-fire, far from embarrassing the United Nations has suffered a diplomatic disaster as great as that over the Cuban missile crisis. As for President Nasser, after years of sensibly cautioning prudence and patience on his Arab brethren, he suddenly overestimated his strength and lost the match.

*   *   *

Her military victory has saved Israel, but the one true victory would be peace. Is something better going to emerge this time, from 'the blood, sweat and tears', than hatred still fanned by humiliation? We must hope against hope that it will.

Local Crisis or World Crisis?[1]

The events of recent weeks in the Middle East will have such grave and lasting consequences that it is vital to analyse as rigorously as possible the conduct of all the participants, big and small.

One of the most common interpretations is that of 'Russian-American connivance'. I have heard this expression several times in the mouths of commentators from outlying vantage-points and M. André Fontaine, in *Le Monde*, has tried hard to prove that the Middle Eastern crisis is not a fresh episode in the cold war. Now, I find these formulas dangerous because they contain a half-truth.

It is legitimate to talk about 'Russian-American connivance' in debates about the non-proliferation of atomic weapons because, in this instance, the two Great Powers have a common interest and are aiming at the same objective. The Middle East is quite another matter. Their supposed 'connivance' is nothing more than the determination not to come directly to blows. This common determination prompted both the Russians and Americans to counsel moderation on President Nasser; it also prompted the Americans to give the same advice to the Israelis, but it did not stop the Russians sending increasing quantities of arms to the Arab States, nor did it stop them heightening the effect of General Rabin's remarks by announcing the build-up of Israeli forces on the Syrian frontier, a build-up that was not confirmed by observers from the United Nations.

At the present time the Soviet Union is not seeking to spread, at least in a primary phase, either its ideas or its regime, and if

[1] Published in the *Figaro*, June 19, 1967.

we lend an essentially ideological character to the cold war there
is no longer any apparent connection between this local crisis and
world politics. But since 1947, as well as being ideological the
cold war has always been a competition between great powers.
Now, this rivalry is less ideological than it was fifteen years ago
(or, let us say, ideology seems more and more to be an instrument of diplomacy) but it has not thereby vanished; there is still
enough of it left to keep the two Great Powers from any joint
action aimed at stabilizing the situation in the Middle East. The
more complex and more agonizing truth is that the ambiguous
relations between the Soviet Union and the United States paralyse any settlement either by force or diplomacy. They will
paralyse it even more in the near future since the Soviet Union,
in order to make the Arabs forget that it was not prepared to
fight for them, will testify before the United Nations in language
all the more fiery and warlike.

At the same time it is true that the decisions which led to the
explosion, President Nasser's in the first place, then those of the
Israeli government, were taken by local actors against the advice
of their respective protectors. The Soviet Union and the United
States were both equally afraid of a conflagration, the first because it did not have the wherewithal for a military intervention,
the second because they did not want to alienate the Arab world
once and for all.

The Great Powers were not in control of things. Nasser issued
a challenge that was too aggressive for the liking of one side,
the Israeli government took up the Egyptian challenge too
brutally for the liking of the other. Even without the Great
Powers Arabs and Israelis would find it hard to coexist peaceably,
but the desire for influence displayed by Russia, the deliveries of
arms and the support by some of the Israeli case have added an
extra dimension to the local conflict.

Here again, any one-sided interpretation would be false: the
two simplified pictures that are painted – either of the Great
Powers manipulating the small ones like marionettes, or else the
small powers fighting to the death despite the wisdom of the
Great ones – are both equally far from the truth. I ask my
readers to forgive me, but it is the reality itself which defies any
crude formalization by its complexity.

The relations between the Great Powers and the small, such as they have shown themselves during these tragic weeks, are also going to be examined with anxious attention by commentators in other countries. In order to express myself, for once, quite bluntly, I shall say that both Arabs and Israelis have the feeling that they were betrayed.

At the moment when Sharm-el-Sheik was being evacuated in 1957, John Foster Dulles had given his solemn promise that the United States would not stand for any new blockade of Eilat. President Johnson honoured his predecessor's promise only verbally. From this the Israeli government has learned to be sceptical of the worth of alliances and pledges. On June 6, faced with the choice between open intervention and an Israeli victory, the Soviet leaders chose the second of these alternatives. Both sides will be disposed to rely more on themselves and less on other people.

*   *   *

Away from the Middle East, are the non-nuclear countries not going to be led, rightly or wrongly, to ask questions about the conditions of their own security? Admittedly, there exists one basic difference between American commitment with regard to Europe and Japan on the one hand, and Israel on the other hand. In the first two instances that commitment is symbolized by the physical presence of American troops. A section of American infantrymen would have saved Sharm-el-Sheik.

If we allow this interpretation then we must conclude that, in the nuclear age, a physical presence alone can make dissuasion effective by forestalling a *fait accompli*. Must the Great Powers then distribute army units around the world in order to inspire confidence in their words? Or, a darker prospect still, must non-nuclear countries eschew all subtlety and seek security in the aquisition of nuclear weapons? How is India, for example, going to react to China's thermonuclear bomb?

In either hypothesis, there is a strong risk that the lessons of the third Middle East war will add to the fears of humanity.

Between Cabinets[1]

On May 24, during the first phase of the Middle East crisis, General de Gaulle proposed to the Great Powers directly concerned in the crisis that they should 'get together'. This was how, up until 1914, the Great Powers had tried to arbitrate forcibly so as to avoid the worst. The President of the United States, who had no clear idea what to do, was quick to accept the French proposal which, obviously, was brushed aside by the Soviet leaders. In all probability the latter did not want hostilities to start but having, in many different ways, encouraged President Nasser, they could not lend themselves to any apparent collusion with the 'imperialists' at the very moment when they were hoping for a diplomatic success by their Arab protégés.

The formula of a 'concert between great powers' belongs to diplomatic tradition. The Soviet Union, Great Britain, France and the United States have, certainly, one characteristic in common: they all possess atomic weapons. If People's China were to occupy the fifth permanent seat on the Security Council the five members of the Atomic Club would also be the five permanent members of the Security Council. One would need, however, to be extremely optimistic or wilfully blind to put France and Great Britain into the same category as the Soviet Union and the United States. The author of *The Edge of the Sword* is the last man to have any illusions on that score and to imagine that words can replace deeds or moral prestige do instead of physical means.

If Europe were involved, a summit meeting of the Four Powers would be something more than a fiction. In the Middle East you have, on the one hand, the local actors, Israel and the Arab countries, on the other the two Great Powers with, per-

[1] June 28, 1967.

haps, in the background, the menacing shadow of China. The European Economic Community was concerning itself with beetroot during these historic days.

Whether it was a twosome or a foursome, the 'concert' of the Great Powers came too late, after the crucial days between May 19 and 22, during which President Nasser had taken the decisions that set the infernal machine in motion. The relations between the White House and the Kremlin hardly allowed President Johnson to explain to Mr Kosygin the predictable sequel to events. The American President had only two choices: either he could let President Nasser know secretly and in advance that he would not stand for the Gulf of Aqaba being closed, or else he could tolerate the blockade and promise Israel diplomatic support. He chose the second alternative.

On May 24, General de Gaulle had invited the Four Powers to 'act in concert'. On June 2, at the next meeting of the Cabinet, a text drawn up by the President of the Republic stated explicitly that: 'France considers that the worst thing would be that hostilities should start. Consequently, the country which first resorts to arms, wherever it may be, would have neither her approval nor, with greater reason, her support.' In between the two meetings of the French cabinet, the Minister of Defence of the United Arab Republic had gone to Moscow, President Nasser had talked in a speech about the destruction of Israel, Algeria had sent troops to the Middle East, King Hussein had made it up with President Nasser and agreed that in case of war his army should be under Egyptian command. In short, two or three more *casus belli* had been added to the blockade of Eilat. General de Gaulle's advance condemnation of the Israeli action could not have had any influence on the events themselves; if the American counsel of moderation had not been heeded in Jerusalem, why should that of France? Any observer of the Middle East knew, on June 2, that a battle had become inevitable.

*   *   *

Three weeks go by and then General de Gaulle, dramatically and in his own unique style, lets it be known what he thinks of the situation in the Middle East and in the world. This time it is no longer a question of the 'concert of the Great Powers'. The cause of all the trouble is the war in Vietnam, 'set off by American intervention'. Even China's exertions to arm herself with nuclear weapons (or at least her haste to do so) can be put down to the war in Vietnam. Does this war also carry the responsibility for French 'haste'?

There may exist a connection between the war in Vietnam and the Middle East crisis. This has seemed to me a plausible hypothesis right from the start, but only the Russians would be in a position either to confirm or deny it. But even if this connection exists, or in other words, even if the Soviet leaders wanted to cause embarrassment to the American leaders by stirring up trouble in a sensitive quarter of the diplomatic field – which is neither excluded nor proven – the fact remains that the Soviet Union has been arming the Arab countries and that it wants to acquire positions and influence in the region in terms of its own national interests, whether there is a war in Vietnam or not. As for the hostility between Arabs and Jews, that preceded the Vietnam war and will, alas, long outlive it.

*   *   *

According to the French President, only some new factor could allow us to hope for a peaceful settlement in the Middle East. Thus, during the last century, France and Great Britain, in the style of the great powers of the past, based their agreement on bargaining; they set limits on their respective spheres of influence, swapped Egypt for Morocco and exchanged goods that did not belong to them. It is to be hoped and indeed it is possible that the Soviet Union and the United States will make concessions to each other here and there, in order to make a better climate for peaceful coexistence. But the very next day after the President of the French Republic had solemnly proclaimed that nothing could be done before the Vietnam war had been brought to an end, Mr Kosygin had long discussions with President Johnson and found the conversation so interesting that he asked for a second meeting. Had the French President hoped to prevent the tête-à-tête between Russia and America? Why was he being more royalist than the kings of the Kremlin?

What struck observers was the caution displayed by the two Great Powers, and their common desire not to fight each other. Whatever be the respective importance of local and general causes in originating the crisis, this desire is typical of international relations as they have been developing in the past twenty years. There are therefore reasons for hoping, luckily, that the 'process presently under way', to repeat the phrase used by a French minister, will not lead to a third world war.

One is far rather tempted to fear not the spectre of a general war but the widespread conviction that nuclear weapons make such a war impossible. Men are getting used not to the idea of a big war, but to the reality of little ones, which may not be on the scale of a nuclear catastrophe but are horrible just the same. We all want the Vietnam war to end, but is the most effective way of doing so to demand an American surrender, that is to go one better than even the Russians themselves? Is it an indispensable part of the politics of independence and neutrality to make haughty moral judgments on those whom General de Gaulle refers to as cold-blooded monsters, that is other countries? Is this helping to achieve peace?

Arms and Peace[1]

Israel could have lost the shooting war, she cannot win it. She has won *a* military victory, but not *the* victory. A State of two and a half million inhabitants has not got the wherewithal to force the Arab countries as a whole to capitulate. She has destroyed two armies, but she has not destroyed either the States or the populations against which she was fighting.

This lack of symmetry partly explains the course of events; it also contains lessons for the future. Whether in the short or the long term, the only true victory for Israel would be peace. Her first objective is to gain recognition from the Arab States, her distant objective remains and must remain reconciliation. This self-evident proposition still does not enable the Israeli leaders to lay down a line of conduct. But it does constitute a warning against illusions and against being carried away by emotion.

In the immediate future, much will depend on the decisions taken in the Kremlin. The Soviet deliveries of tanks and fighter planes to Egypt were predictable and are normal. They in no way prove that Moscow's leaders are contemplating an imminent renewal of hostilities. Whatever happened, these leaders had to support President Nasser and, since they either could or would not intervene militarily at the critical moment, they were morally and politically bound to replace the material that had been destroyed, at least in part.

The real questions go beyond this. A fourth encounter, after those of 1948, 1956 and 1967, would make no sense for the Russians or the Egyptians without profound modifications in certain military factors. The shock effect of armoured divisions in the desert favours the army that is the more mobile, the more able to manoeuvre quickly, whose soldiers are better trained and

[1] July 5, 1967.

whose commanders are, at every level, better at taking the initiative.

The Arabs will become, just as other nations, technologically proficient. If, as François Mauriac has written, Shylock has turned back into King David, it would be both monstrous and absurd to substitute an anti-Arab anti-semitism for an anti-Jewish anti-semitism, and to forge an image of the Arab eternally dedicated to poverty and to menial tasks. But the modernization of an army presupposes the modernization of a society; both take time.

In the years to come (I am not talking in terms of decades), the Egyptians would only have a chance of military success against Israel if they received a different sort of help from the Russians: either a considerably augmented number of Soviet advisers, or the participation of 'volunteers' from Socialist countries, or else a resort to long-range weapons (ballistic missiles). If the Russians and Egyptians were to embark on this path the Israelis would be forced not to allow themselves to be outpaced in the arms race.

Happily, the worst is still not certain. The Egyptians will hesitate before a choice that would imprison them completely within the Soviet alliance, while the rulers of the Kremlin will not perhaps launch themselves on an adventure at the end of which looms a direct confrontation with the United States. It is thus at least possible that, during the coming phase, the Egyptians will accept the existence of Israel and that the Russians, while consolidating their position in the Middle East, will abstain from egging the Arabs on to a new trial of strength.

Let us suppose that this optimistic hypothesis is borne out: in that case it would be both the duty and in the interests of the government in Jerusalem to help those Arab leaders ready to take the responsibility for an unpopular policy. It can only help them by moderation, by resisting the temptation to seek security on the map, by making frontiers coincide with rivers. In the long term, one or two decades hence, it is not a Jordanian army that will constitute a threat to Tel Aviv, but the installation of medium-range missiles in Egypt or Syria. The best way of countering this danger is to hold out a hand to those Arabs who have not refused it once and for all.

There are three hundred thousand Arabs inside the State of Israel. Even if this minority does benefit from a standard of living equal or superior to that of the Arabs in Syria or Jordan, it is deprived of the essential: the Arabs are not full citizens of the Israeli State; as second-rate citizens they form a semi-foreign body. The Jews of Israel, who themselves experienced the same misfortune for so long, cannot help but understand the feelings of this minority. Otherwise we would have to conclude, with bitter resignation, that the monotonous and tragic sequence of injustice and oppression will continue into the future, for as far as the eye is able to pierce the mists.

Since the Arab countries refused to recognize Israel's existence, the latter could neither trust the loyalty of the Arab minority nor agree to the massive reflux of the Palestinian victims of the 1948 crisis. Tomorrow conditions may be different. But a Transjordania that was an Israeli protectorate would be just as unacceptable to the Arabs as an Israel that was an Arab protectorate would be to the Jews.

Mere cooperation in the Middle East between Israelis and Arabs, the prospect of which may be vaguely taking shape, requires the consent of Palestinians and Jordanians. This will not be prised out by force of arms.

Why?[1]

A few weeks ago, I told one of my friends who was indignant at a communiqué handed to the papers on the day after a cabinet meeting: 'You'll see worse, I bet you France will vote for the motion supported by Russia at the United Nations.' It gives me no pleasure to have been such a good prophet. My interpretation of the person and the mental processes of General de Gaulle prompted me to predict the diplomatic slide out of neutrality and into solidarity with the Arab countries and the Soviet Union. But today, quite dispassionately, I ask myself: why?

A motion that called on the Israelis to evacuate the territories conquered by their armies before any settlement and without any guarantees, would not have been obeyed by the government in Jerusalem. It would, on the other hand, have given the Arab countries and the Soviet Union an additional reason for being intransigent, the hope of winning back by diplomacy what had been compromised on the field of battle. If the aim of French diplomacy is to favour a lasting solution, the least that can be said is that France's conversion to the Soviet/Arab theses does not seem conducive to this end.

Let us allow that, in order to display its spirit of fair play to the Arabs, our government was right not to honour the commitments entered into by the French government in 1957 concerning the Gulf of Aqaba. Let us admit too that it had good reason, both before and after the hostilities, to express its disapproval of the resort to arms. Harder to accept are the communiqué on the cabinet meeting of June 21, where even the appearance of objectivity, in respect of the United States as much as of Israel, has vanished, the French vote in the United Nations and even more perhaps the attempt of the French delegation to convince

[1] July 7, 1967.

our friends in black Africa to vote with the Soviet Union (what do they think deep down, these men who are professional servants of the State, that is, these days, of one man?).

Let us talk the language of pure realism. Those States in black Africa whose leaders are moderates were worried or indignant. The Russian deliveries of arms to Algeria and the so-called revolutionary policy of M. Boumedienne caused great misgiving in Tunis and Rabat, whose rulers could understand France's neutrality but not the pro-Soviet 'militancy', the support given, knowingly and deliberately, to all those in the Third World who professed the most hostile feelings towards the Americans and the West.

Is it going to be said that General de Gaulle thereby succeeded in removing France from the hostility vowed by the Arab and a number of Asiatic and African countries to 'American imperialism' or to 'Western imperialism'? In order to display her independence and dissociate herself from American policy in Vietnam, there is no need for France to be more Russian than the Russians. Whether she likes it or not, France belongs to Europe, to the family of rich countries, and her social order is thoroughly conservative.

In spite of everything, the diplomatic games the President of the Republic has been indulging in, his indifference to ideologies and to countries' internal regimes, his switching of alliances, seem to me anachronistic. Such supreme realism brings short-term benefits but it also involves a reckoning which, as I see it, far exceeds this temporary profit.

Opinion both in France and outside will in the end grasp the least glorious aspect of this sort of diplomacy. In 1960, General de Gaulle received Mr Ben Gurion as the representative of a country that was a friend and an ally. In 1967, Israel, which owes its armaments to France, has the feeling of having been treated as an enemy by this same General de Gaulle: are all friends of the United States enemies of France? Are the enemies of the Soviet or Arab revolutionaries also enemies of France? Is there anything to be gained by a country of only limited resources earning the reputation that Great Britain enjoyed in the last century, of having only interests and no friends?

France has broken away both from her partners in the Common Market and from the other countries in the Atlantic area, or in other words she has broken with those to whom she is the most closely tied by her economy, her culture and her ideals. Is it sufficient compensation to receive a tribute from President Tito's Yugoslavia?

If the French moves had helped to bring about peace, then this so-called realistic calculation of profit and loss would not, in the last resort, have had any bearing. But, in point of fact, everything has happened as if General de Gaulle's overriding objective was either always and everywhere to oppose the United States, or else to provoke the Soviet leaders to extremism. Nothing could be more normal than that General de Gaulle should condemn the war in Vietnam, which is condemned by the vast majority of European opinion. What is surprising is that he should talk and act as if he preferred a continuation of the conflict to a compromise, as if he was hoping less for peace than an American defeat, as if he feared above all else an agreement between the Russians and the Americans. Yet in March 1949, de Gaulle, who was then the president of the Rassemblement du Peuple Français, declared at a press conference: 'I know very well that some weak-spirited people aspire, as they say, to replace strength by policy. But no policy, even and especially one of great generosity, has ever been formed once strength has been renounced. In Indo-China, some people advocate what they call the Ho Chi-minh solution, that is, in actual fact, surrender.'

*   *   *

Ever since the Middle East crisis began, I had had the feeling that the President of the Republic would be led by the logic of his diplomacy to join the Soviet camp. But today I ask myself with anguish: was it still a logic of the reason or simply a logic of the emotions? Does the anti-American obsession of the present not resemble the anti-English obsession of Vichy in 1940?

Israel between War and Peace[1]

In their newly published book on *The Six Day War* Randolph and Winston Churchill, the son and grandson of Sir Winston, record this comment by an Israeli paratrooper: 'This is an interesting country, never a moment's boredom. A war breaks out, it's over in six days and you've turned the whole world upside down.'

At the end of a short stay in Israel and reading the Churchills' book, I asked myself: has the world really been turned upside down?

By its brutality Israel's victory in the field surprised, not the heads of the Israeli Air Force or the experts in the Pentagon, but at least most outside politicians, not to mention probably the Soviet intelligence services. But to win a battle is still not to win the war. The Arab leaders have proclaimed as much, repeating a formula that has already gone down in history: the Arabs have lost a battle – the third in twenty years – they haven't lost the war.

Let us beware of paradox, however. Everything hasn't changed, but there is a new element. The political impasse remains, but it is no longer the same.

*　　*　　*

Henceforth no one is in any doubt that the Israeli army is the strongest in the Middle East, without a rival for as long as the Soviet Union does not intervene directly or send in Muslim 'volunteers'. The presence of the American Sixth Fleet in the Eastern Mediterranean makes any intervention improbable in

[1] August 28, 1967.

the near future contravening the normal rules of Russian diplomacy.

Some Israeli generals amongst those at the top believed that the balance of forces had become less favourable by 1967 than it had been in 1965. They have now found out that the margin of superiority had in fact grown not narrower but wider.

Admittedly, thanks to the destruction on the ground, within a few hours, of the greater part of the Egyptian Air Force, the Israeli infantry and armoured divisions enjoyed a decisive advantage. More than any other sort of warfare, tank warfare in the desert is influenced by air strikes. Yet, whatever the role of surprise and the effectiveness of her Mystères and Mirages, Israel's superiority asserted itself on all sorts of terrain and in every form of fighting.

Not that the Egyptian, Jordanian and Syrian troops did not fight bravely. Nor were their officers and NCOs without the technical knowledge needed to handle modern weapons. If the people I spoke to in Jerusalem and Tel Aviv are to be believed, what the Arab armies lack above all is social integration, without which there can be no collective action. A 'unit', whether a section or a whole army, only exists on condition that the men have confidence in one another. Not all the Egyptian officers knew the names of their own men and were surprised at the surprise their Israeli questioners showed when they learned of this.

The Israelis, for their part, were relieved to discover that on the day of their ordeal they were united, despite their partisan quarrels. Eastern Jews and Western Jews, Sephardim Jews and Ashkenazim Jews, although they do not occupy the same position in the social hierarchy, together made up a nation. At least for a time, the racial tensions that have often been strong in recent years were relaxed in the awareness of a common destiny and a shared danger. (The Egyptian and Syrian propaganda, which so many Israelis were able to listen to, since their mother tongue is Arabic, completed the work of civic education done by the army.)

As for the return of the Israelis into Jerusalem, the event has such significance for the faithful of three religions, it raises such emotions, pure and impure, political and mystical, in the subconscious of Christians, Muslims and Jews, that an observer is afraid of missing the main point the moment he limits himself to the language of reason and unbelief. Yet he cannot forget the remark of a pious Israeli friend, a practising Jew: 'And now the Muslims and not only the Arabs will see us as enemies.' The remarks of the Chief Rabbi of the Army, about the reconstruction of the Temple and praying by the Holy Places of the Muslims, have been retracted by the man who made them, but not perhaps forgotten by those most intimately affected by them.

A defeat for Russia, a victory for the Americans, it has been said. Is the balance-sheet such a simple one? The Russians were anxious about the fragility of the Syrian regime, the most 'progressive' and the closest, in tone and in action, to the Socialist camp. Despite or because of the defeat, this regime has perhaps been strengthened, in so far as it now has a greater need than ever of its mighty protector. Egypt too now has less room for manoeuvre than before. During the last two months she has received from the Soviet Union fighter planes (but no bombers) and tanks, which will make up, so they say, for between 50 and 75 per cent of the losses suffered. These deliveries of arms do not, of course, herald any aggressive intent for the near future. The Russians could not but rearm President Nasser, if only to restore his prestige and authority. If their objective was to acquire military bases in the Eastern Mediterranean or to turn a few Arab countries into people's democracies, then they are closer to achieving it after the defeat of their allies than they were before. But do they want to shoulder the economic burden of Egypt, which is heavily in debt and whose President may tomorrow, as he did yesterday, take chancy decisions off his own bat?

As for the American President, his first reaction to the Six Day War was satisfaction. His predecessor had signed, over the Gulf of Aqaba, solemn pledges which he himself did not want to go back on but did not know how to honour. The Israelis undertook to solve his problem for him.

What now? The principles of the settlement proclaimed by President Johnson preclude a return to the *statu quo ante*, but would the Arabs agree to pay, in Israel's recognizance, for the evacuation of the conquered territories? And would the Israelis agree to evacuate the conquered territories in exchange for nothing but an international guarantee whose flimsiness they were able to gauge in May 1967? In New York, the Russians and Americans agreed on a text which the Arabs have rejected and which the Israelis would only have accepted conditionally. Neither of the two Great Powers has any way of exacting obedience from their respective protégés any longer. Now, as before, both Israelis and Arabs are little inclined to conclude a real peace, even if they are also loath to start another real war.

Is the outcome of the local hostilities going to be once again to substitute one cease-fire for another, and a continuation of what Mao Tse-tung calls 'prolonged conflict'? Even in that case, two events, one pregnant with history, the other with geopolitics or geoeconomics would still be significant. The Muslims have lost their sovereignty over the Holy Places, and there is a risk that the decline of the Suez Canal, which may stay closed for a long time, is henceforth irremediable.

A Diplomacy in Search of a Policy[1]

'*Embarras de richesses*' one of the leaders of the Republic of Israel said to me with an ambiguous smile. 'Jerusalem, the Gaza strip, Sinai, the West bank of the Jordan. This time we hold the best cards; it's up to the others to ask themselves what course to follow.'

I interrupted the minister: 'Are you stressing the embarrassment or the riches? If you mean cards to negotiate with then you have plenty. If you hang on to your conquests, would they be riches?'

The minister was ready to admit that these riches risked becoming a source of embarrassment in the future. But he was careful not to speculate on what would happen in the case where 'the consequences of the aggression are not eliminated', to use the language of Soviet diplomacy. He outlined the well-known theses of Israeli diplomacy, insisting on guarantees of security.

This dialogue, which is neither fictive nor symbolic, is an indication of the present predicament. The Israelis still know what they have to say. At times they know what they hope to obtain. They do not know what they will do if they do not obtain it. Perhaps even, they still do not know what they are hoping for deep down.

Leaders and opinion alike are finding it hard fully to grasp what has taken place and what has happened to them. On the morning of June 5, Mr Levi Eshkol sent a message to King Hussein, begging him not to intervene. It was not until the end of the morning, after the Jordanians had captured the building occupied by the United Nations, that the commander of the

[1] Published in the *Figaro*, August 29, 1967.

Central Front received the order to attack. Today Jerusalem is one city and Israeli soldiers hold the bank of the Jordan and the Suez Canal.

But there is another side to it: 300,000 1948 refugees are still living in the Gaza Strip, maintained by a special fund of the United Nations. The Palestinians in the strip and those on the West bank of the Jordan together make up about a million people, to be added to the 300,000 Arabs contained within the 1949 frontiers of the State of Israel. This State contains less than two and a half million Jews, reproducing themselves less fast than the Arab minority which votes but does not carry arms.

What is to be done? Different factions have formed inside the government as well as in public opinion. If we attribute fixed ideas to parties and persons, we can draw up a picture that would be as satisfying to the mind as it is far removed from reality.

To start with we must dismiss a first school which includes a few writers or publicists of quality, but is not represented in the ruling circles. This first school we shall call that of the multi-racial secular State. Arabs and Jews are both Semites, made to live at one and not to fight, still less to rally to the opposing camps confronting one another on a world scale, who subordinate the interests of the Middle East to external interests and to the mathematics of a global diplomacy. Treat the Arabs as equals and make a basic distinction between the Jewish religion and the State of Israel and our action, our example, will gradually make possible something beyond coexistence: cooperation and then a federation of those nations today pledged to a war ruinous for all of them.

Such a programme assumes that the problem has been resolved. Even those Jews who are not religious remain wedded to an essentially Jewish State. The unbelieving Ashkenazim who left Europe to go back to the Promised Land preserve the awareness of a Hebraic identity. Many are acquainted with Arab civilization, all dream of restoring peace, but for them the Arabs will still be 'the others' for a long time to come. The latter, for their part, even if they do enjoy a higher standard of living than their brethren over the border, will feel themselves aliens in a State that only grants them half-rights as citizens.

If a multi-racial State without discrimination between Arabs

4

and Jews remains impossible for the time being, and the Israelis have few illusions on that score, is not the ruthless conclusion an alternative whose two terms seem almost equally unacceptable? Either they can evacuate the conquered territories, or in any case the West bank of the Jordan, or else they can become what their enemies have been accusing them of being for years, the last colonizers, the last wave of Western imperialism.

The above alternative expresses the conclusion, one might almost say the philosophy, of the Israelis' dialogue with themselves, their friends and their enemies. But before it comes to that there are distinctions to be made.

Jerusalem is no longer, in the official phrase, an 'object of negotiation'. The former partitioning of the town was contrary to the nature of things, its present unification marks a return to order, if it is possible to talk about a natural order in these lands, whose destination is religious and whose destiny, over the centuries, has been to serve as a thoroughfare for conquerors and as a battlefield for combatants, some in search of sacred relics, others carried away by imperial ambition.

The Gaza Strip also constitutes a separate problem. The refugees had not left their camps. The Palestinians in the strip were subjected to an Egyptian administration, but not treated as Egyptian citizens; they needed a permit to go into Egypt. The Israeli authorities are striving less to recruit *collaborators* than to urge the Palestinians to administer themselves. A wholly temporary solution since it does not, theoretically, prejudge the issue of sovereignty. But there are considerations of security involved too. It is unthinkable, some people tell me, that the Gaza Strip, on Israel's border, should once again serve as an advance post for an Egyptian army. Demilitarize it then? Perhaps, but what are promises worth? Bring it under Israeli rule? But leaving aside the refugees, the Palestinians of Gaza will swell even further the Arab minority in Israel.

The Sinai desert is the most favourable battlefield for the Israeli army, the most dangerous for the Egyptian army. It is hard to believe that the latter would use it for a fourth round. The argument over security should not prevent a compromise, despite the objections of the pilots, who are anxious to have a few extra minutes in hand to alert the rest of their defences.

There remains the essential point: the West bank of the Jordan, pregnant with memories of Jewish history but lived on by Palestinians, who were not perhaps devoted to the Hashemite dynasty but who are, however the Israeli troops may behave, experiencing the humiliation and resentment of all occupied populations. They are more Palestinian than Arab, declare some Israelis. Let us allow them to administer themselves, let us grant them technical aid. Jordan was an artificial creation of the mandatory power. In a few years' time the answer will be taking shape progressively on the ground: autonomous province, associate State, Israeli-Jordanian confederation, no one can settle it in advance. Let us act as we have always done; measuring not hopes against possibilities but possibilities against our will.

The Palestinians of Transjordania are still Arabs, whatever their pecularities, say others. The Israeli presence will fan the flames of Arab nationalism. We shall enter on the infernal cycle of occupation and repression. We shall betray ourselves by violating the moral principle on which our State is based. Like all Western colonialists in the twentieth century we shall afterwards have guilty consciences. The moral danger is greater than the military danger of restoring Transjordania to Jordanian sovereignty. As for the solution of an *independent* Transjordania, but with Israeli troops along the Jordan, that is equivalent to setting up a protectorate in the precise sense which that term had during the last century.

*   *   *

What do individual Israelis fear the most? The spiritual corruption of the nation by conquest? The military insecurity of evacuating the occupied territories? The loss of their Jewish identity through the expansion of the Arab minority? Were I not obliged to discretion I might reveal in what order each of the people I spoke to placed these various perils, without perhaps themselves being aware of it. But, soldiers and civilians alike, they always came back to a diplomatic formula that cannot be faulted: let the Arabs consent to discuss a peace settlement and anything would be possible.

For want of agreement among themselves and about their

vocation, the Israelis are holding on to what they have occupied and leaving the responsibility of a choice to the Arabs. The Arab decision will thus in part settle the fate of Israel. For if the present situation is prolonged the occupation regime will create *faits accomplis* in its turn whose duration and consequences no one can foretell.

Will the Arabs Agree to Negotiate?[1]

Having been defeated, are the Arabs prepared to recognize the existence and legitimacy of the State of Israel? I would like to say 'yes'. The Arab-Israeli war has multiplied suffering, it is paralysing the economic development of a whole region, it threatens at every moment to spread, it arouses passions such that, in every country in Europe, East or West, citizens stand opposed to one another and have sometimes been up in arms against the policy of their country.

* * *

A few articles in the Egyptian press give grounds for hope of a change of style and tactics, if not a conversion. For as long as Arab propaganda openly preaches the destruction of the State of Israel – not to mention, in the days preceding the war, the threat to wipe out the men and rape the women – even those Westerners least favourable to Israel cannot fully uphold the Arab cause. As a left-wing intellectual wrote in the 'Tribune Libre' column in *Le Monde*, an Israeli victory was better in the short run, as averting a genocide and safeguarding the future of the two camps.

President Nasser seems to be contemplating a diplomatic settlement of the crisis. Against the extremism of Damascus and Algiers, he has opted for the moderation that had characterized his diplomacy in recent years and from which he suddenly departed in May, 1967, for reasons that are still obscure. But, having been defeated, can he agree to the concessions he refused

[1] August 30, 1967.

before? Can he, even if he wants to, pay the price the Israelis are demanding?

The Suez Canal is closed to shipping. The Israelis are not opposed to it being reopened, but since, according to them, the cease-fire line passes down the middle of the canal, they simply repeat: either Israeli vessels shall have the right to use the Canal or no vessels from any country will use it. Egypt is being deprived of vital revenue, the Soviet Union of a means of communication with the Far East. As time passes the longer the work needed to make the canal usable again will take. The oil companies are now banking on the huge tankers that will go round the Cape. This concession would seem to herald a recognition obstinately withheld for nineteen centuries. Would the hero of Arab nationalism, voted back by plebiscite on the day of disaster, be followed along the road, no longer of battle, but of armistice or even peace? That I do not know.

Where the Canal is concerned, all it needs is a concession whose only significance is symbolic. But when it comes to Jerusalem or to Transjordania, the Israelis are demanding more. The motion on which the Russians and Americans had reached agreement – recognition of the State of Israel in return for the withdrawal of Israeli troops, has been rejected by the Arabs; it would not have been implemented by the Israelis. For the present, one cannot see any Israeli government going back on the unification of Jerusalem, any more than one can see any Arab government renouncing Jerusalem. Politics or religion? Politics and religion inextricably entwined: the fate of the Holy City has once again set Israel against Ishmael, and the Christians, divided among themselves, are not simply spectators.

Agreed, none of these problems is insoluble in itself. Jerusalem will no longer be split into two towns without any form of communication between them. But whether it is a question of the Holy Places or of Jordanian or Palestinian suzerainty over the Arab town, the diplomats are clever enough to work out a formula the moment the politicians entrust them with finding one. The Israeli government may be more ready to do so than we think and than it gives the impression of being. Unfortunately, the one necessary condition is still the most difficult: Israel wants negotiations with each neighbouring State in particular, not with the Arab States as a whole. She would probably make concessions to King Hussein that she would not make either to the United Nations or to the coalition of Arab countries. But can King Hussein, having sacrificed his army to the cause of Arab unity, treat on his own with the common enemy?

At the United Nations, the Arab countries would put Israel in an awkward position if they gave up the arguments they have been upholding since 1949 and resigned themselves to peace. There are many reasons, both moral and material, why they have not resigned themselves to it so far. In the eyes of non-Arabs, to recognize the existence of the State of Israel is to admit a fact; in Arab eyes, it is to accept an injustice and admit a defeat. Whatever our own views, we need to understand them on this.

Moreover, Arab unity, already more a fiction than a reality in the present circumstances, would be further weakened the day Israel ceased to be the absolute enemy. Even in the choice of short-term tactics, extremists and moderates can agree only with difficulty. The most violent statements are now being made in Damascus and Algiers. Admittedly, the longing for unity has been strengthened by a disaster that was felt by every Arab, from Aden to Casablanca. The liquidation of the war in the Yemen and an agreement between Egypt and Saudi Arabia would be both a condition and a confirmation of that unity. For the moment, the conflict of interests persists between traditional regimes and the countries enriched by their petroleum, and the poor countries.

For the time being the Arab countries, like Israel, have taken up diplomatic positions rather than adopted a plan of campaign. Naturally, they want to recover the territories they have lost as cheaply as they can, just as the Israelis want either to keep them or else obtain the maximum advantage from exchanging them. But do the Israelis know whether they ought to ask more than the Arabs can give? Do the Arabs know whether they would prefer to pay a certain price or else force the Israelis to play the role of imperialists by refusing all concessions?

The Arabs have two main courses of action: one economic, the other political and military. If all the Arab states were to conclude a true alliance and act in concert, the petrol embargo would discomfort the West. But this sword has a double edge.

The producer states would ruin themselves while the most powerful of the 'imperialist' states, the United States, would remain unshaken. Great Britain would be hit the hardest by the withdrawal of funds by the Arab countries or the nationalization of the oil companies. Israel would not be affected. The blows struck at the West would not mean that the United States would force Israel to evacuate the occupied territories without something in return.

The political military weapon would be guerrillas. The raids of the *fedayin* originated the crisis of 1956, those of the commandoes from Syria that of 1967. The present lines of demarcation make terrorist incursions from outside more difficult, but the passive resistance in Jerusalem and Transjordania might one day turn into an active resistance.

The Israelis are not afraid of this happening; they believe themselves capable of maintaining order under any circumstances. I shall refrain from expressing an opinion on this point. But, once again, must we not fear the infernal cycle of violence, in which both sides expose themselves to the danger of losing their lives and their reasons for living?

*   *   *

The Six Day War was only one vicissitude in the prolonged conflict that began with the creation of the State of Israel. On this point, Israel and the Arabs are in agreement, which only makes any solution, even a temporary one, more arduous: the former would still not trust the will to peace of the latter even on the day they extracted from them the recognition they have been demanding in vain since 1948. Now, the search for military security at all costs contains within it contradictions and a malediction. In a violent world no security is absolute. The security of one entails the insecurity of another and all experience the martyrdom of Sisyphus.

In its next phase, the conflict ought to unfold on the terrain of diplomacy and economics. But if it is prolonged there is a risk of it one day acquiring a new dimension: above the traditional weapons there are atomic weapons and ballistic missiles, below them the bombs and machine-guns of the partisans.

Intervention of the Powers?[1]

A less incomplete analysis of the situation in the Middle East would have meant asking questions in Moscow, Washington and the Arab capitals. The desires, ambitions and dreams of the Israelis form only one element in one of the most complex diplomatic puzzles of the postwar period.

Yet in the short term it so happens that the Middle East constitutes a relatively autonomous system, by the fact that the great powers have rendered one another incapable of movement there. Thus some Israelis, concerned purely with the threat that hangs over them and conscious of their strength, are becoming almost indifferent about the deliberations at the United Nations and the world's judgments, being convinced both that their security depends above all on themselves alone and that they have in any case acquired the protection of the United States.

These two propositions were confirmed by the experience of 1967, but that does not make them true once and for all.

* * *

The Israelis are not afraid of American pressure forcing them to make major concessions. During the weeks preceding hostilities, the memory of Eisenhower's policy in 1956 hung over the ministerial deliberations; it explains in part the government's hesitations. In actual fact, the situation in 1967 seemed quite different from what it was in 1956; this time there was no collusion with powers outside the Middle East, fighting not for their lives but for their interests.

[1] August 31, 1967.

Would the war have happened if Israel had not attacked first? The Egyptians, Syrians, Jordanians and Iraqis had, at all events, stepped up their provocations. Within her 1949 frontiers Israel could not, without risk of extinction, allow her neighbours to take the initiative, to choose their own moment and their own terrain.

In his speeches, even as he denounced *Israeli aggression*, President Nasser admitted that he had challenged the enemy by closing the Straits of Tiran, by massing his troops in Sinai and patching things up in spectacular fashion with King Hussein, who placed his troops under Egyptian command, even as Iraqi divisions were entering Jordan.

In 1967, opinion both in the United States and in Western Europe was massively behind the Israeli cause. Even in Eastern Europe many, and not all of them Jews, in Poland, Czechoslovakia and the Soviet Union, hoped for an Israeli victory despite the attitudes adopted by the governments of the Socialist camp.

That opinion is changing. Israel no longer appears as David confronting Goliath. It is the Arabs who have been struck down and who are experiencing the worst of afflictions, that of a collective humiliation. The fickleness of public opinion matters less than that of the chancelleries. In June 1967, the United States and the Soviet Union agreed not to intervene directly, and so first to limit the conflict, then to stop it. Will they agree to impose a solution?

*   *   *

General de Gaulle must have told the Israeli Foreign Minister that no settlement was possible in the Middle East without the participation of Moscow.

This analysis surprised the Israelis without convincing them. Of course, if the Soviet Union had suddenly changed its attitude and accepted the existence of Israel within her 1949 frontiers, the concerted action of the two Great Powers might perhaps have forced both Arabs and Israelis to submit to peace conditions that both have rejected equally. But the remarks made in private by Eastern European diplomats prior to the Six Day War, suggested nothing of the kind. They were interested in a return to the partition plan of 1947, which the Israelis had accepted at the time and the Arabs rejected, but which, in the present circumstances, no longer has anything more than a historical interest.

The formula of a 'concert of the Great Powers' belongs to the pre-1914 world. In not a single instance since 1945 have the Big Two or the Big Four, or the United Nations, been able really to get to the heart of the matter. Whether it was Korea, Kashmir or Berlin, the problems have either ripened or gone bad; they have not been solved by the 'concert of the world'.

* * *

United States diplomacy has come out against a pure and simple return to the situation of May, 1967. It has not given any concrete definition of the conditions of the settlement it is hoping for, nor of the limits that it would eventually set on the extension of Israel's territory. It wants manifestly to resume economic and political relations with those Arab States with traditional regimes which produce oil. It even wants to divert President Nasser from committing himself finally to the Socialist camp. But for as long as the Arab countries do not choose between an armistice and war, it is being careful not to intervene actively or to exert pressure on Israel. In Washington the watchword still seems to be: there is an urgent need to wait. Perhaps, after all, one of Israel's neighbouring States will make up its mind to do a deal.

There is no doubt at all that the United States contemplates bringing the Soviet Union into any negotiated settlement so as to strengthen the 'doves' in the Kremlin and to symbolize the fact that peaceful coexistence is still with us despite the Vietnam war. Will American and Russian collusion go to the point of dictating peace conditions to both sides? I think not.

The Soviet Union bears a share of the responsibility for the events of June, 1967. No one knows what Mr Gromyko said to President Nasser in March, 1967 when he was in Cairo. But two facts remain: the delivery of considerable quantities of arms, and the false report of the build-up of Israeli troops along the frontier with Syria, and the Soviet Ambassador's rejection of the offer made to him by Mr Levi Eshkol to go and make an on-the-spot inspection.

Soviet diplomacy probably thought that the Syrian regime was in danger after the air battle on April 7, in which six Syrian MIGs were shot down. The build-up of Egyptian troops in Sinai, following the defence agreement between Egypt and Syria, was aimed in any case at dissuading the Jerusalem government from any more acts of reprisal. Israeli specialists, however, continue to hesitate between two interpretations: either a plan aimed at consolidating the pro-Russian regimes in Syria and Egypt before the troubles that will inevitably follow the relinquishment by the British of their last possessions in South Arabia, or else a succession of more or less improvised movements in answer to situations not properly understood. On one point these two interpretations coincide: the Russians neither wanted hostilities to commence, nor did they approve in advance President Nasser's rash decisions.

For the time being the Russian position in the Arab countries has been maintained or consolidated. But these days an expansion of political power normally brings with it an increase in the economic burden. Grandeur costs money and brings in nothing. Egypt is not paying as much for Russian MIGs as Israel pays for French Mirages. She is even less able today to pay for either her debts or her armaments. Moscow's objective is obviously to 'wipe out the traces of Israeli aggression', to bring about the evacuation of the occupied territories without excessive expense or renewed risks. The Kremlin can, at a pinch, rely on Washington to tone down Israeli ambition and to forbid annexations which would make the Soviet Union lose face. But that is all. Russian/American collusion would only perhaps become effective if Arab diplomacy were to undergo a conversion, a conversion which the Israelis both hope for and fear at one and the same time.

*   *   *

As for France, where opinion was pro-Israeli and whose government apparently pro-Arab, she, thanks to this spontaneous division of labour, has kept sympathies in both camps. But between now and the end of the year, the President of the Republic must take a grave decision: whether or not to lift the embargo on the aeroplanes already ordered and paid for by Israel. If the embargo is not quickly lifted, Israel will renounce her special relationship with the French arms industry. (The Israelis think French aircraft the best in the world.) At the same time she would lose the narrow margin of manoeuvre in respect of the United States guaranteed her by France's friendship. One more country would have been handed over lock, stock and barrel to the 'American hegemony'.

France appears only to have played a minor role in the development of the crisis. Yet one of the most famous men in Israel told me that President Nasser would not have decreed the blockade of the Gulf of Aqaba if he had not thought he had the support of France. When I expressed some scepticism, he told me: 'That is not opinion but fact.'

*   *   *

At the United Nations, the Soviet Union sought French co-operation in order to win the French-speaking countries of black Africa over to her cause. But it was with the United States that she drafted a common motion and looked for a settlement. France is today a neutral country and has supplied officers to the commission responsible for seeing that the cease-fire is respected.

These articles of mine reflect imperfectly the state of mind of most Israelis. They have not grown drunk with victory, but their consciences are easy and they feel fewer doubts or anxieties than their friends. They are convinced they fought to save their very existence and they have now, for the most part, gone back to their peacetime occupations, both within Israel and abroad, ready at the first call to resume their uniforms and their arms. The government does not have a policy laid down once and for all, it has a strategy. It is up to the Arabs and above all to Jordan to decide between war and peace. And perhaps neither King Hussein nor President Nasser is powerful enough to choose.

What can the well-intentioned observer do, who has not forgotten the wrong done to the Arabs by the creation of the State of Israel but who is convinced that the destruction of that State would today be an inexpiable crime? As long as the Arab States take as their aim the destruction of Israel, even if they dream of it rather than will it, how can we reject the arguments about security constantly invoked by ministers and generals in Jerusalem and Tel Aviv?

Whenever those with whom I spoke forced me, against my will, to formulate an opinion, I warned them against the snare laid for them less by the enemy than by History. In the long run, there can be no peace without reconciliation. This will not come tomorrow, nor does it depend on the Israelis alone. But the prospect of it, which is in any case a distant one, could be made more remote still by certain decisions made possible by victory.

The UN in the Middle East Crisis[1]

Historians no longer hold back from writing the history of the present. Less than five months have gone by since the Middle East crisis and already the professors are struggling to give an objective account of it. The Institute of Strategic Studies in London has just published a study, under the names of Michael Howard and Robert Hunter, which enables us to revise certain judgments made at the time and which, if it does not bring us any revelations, does summarize what we do and do not know.

One first lesson, it seems to me, comes out of their analysis: the responsibility for the conflict falls, essentially, on the actors of the 'sub-system', on the Arab countries and on Israel, not on the United Nations, the United States or the Soviet Union. Neither U Thant, Messrs Kosygin and Brezhnev, or President Johnson wanted a war they could not prevent.

Most people in the West, including the American President himself, have criticized the behaviour of U Thant. The documents now available have convinced me of the injustice which I, along with many others, committed. It would have been very awkward for U Thant to adopt any other line of conduct. Even some different, Hammarskjöld-type action would probably not have deflected events from their course.

On the evening of May 16, General Rikhye, commanding the UN Peacekeeping Force, received a message from the Egyptian general Fawzy asking the UN troops to withdraw from the frontier. Much more than that, the Egyptian commander expressed verbally another demand: immediate evacuation of the two key posts of El Salha, on the frontier with Sinai and Sharm-el-Sheik on the Straits of Tiran. We still do not know on whose

[1] Published in the *Figaro*, October 26, 1967.

initiative this last demand was made, General Fawzy's or President Nasser's. General Rikhye rejected the Egyptian request on the grounds that it ought to have been made to the Secretary-General of the United Nations.

The next day, May 17, at the end of the morning, the Egyptians asked for a second time that the UN force should be withdrawn, and for a second time its Indian general refused. On the morning of May 18, Egyptian troops forced the Yugoslav units to evacuate their positions at El-Amr and El-Kuntilla. At noon, the commander of the post at Sharm-el-Sheik received and rejected a fifteen-minute ultimatum. On the night of May 18/19, the Secretary-General of the United Nations gave the order to General Rikhye for a general evacuation.

What had been happening in New York meanwhile? As soon as U Thant learned of the Egyptian move on the evening of May 16, he got in touch with Mr El Kony, the permanent representative at the UN of the United Arab Republic. The latter declared he knew nothing of the affair. According to the Secretary-General, a withdrawal, partial or temporary, of the UN forces, from all or part of the border, was inadmissible, since it was the job of these forces to avert conflict and they could not stand passively by at a resumption of hostilities. On the other hand, if the Egyptian government was asking officially for the UN troops to be withdrawn, the international organization would comply with their request. The stationing of UN troops on the territory of a sovereign State presupposes the consent of that State. The United Arab Republic had the right to withdraw the consent given in 1957.

On May 17, the Secretary-General of the United Nations consulted the representatives of the countries providing units for the international force. The representatives of India and Yugoslavia upheld the Egyptian thesis. The representative of Canada took a different position. He predicted, clear-sightedly, the probable consequences of the decision and argued in favour of a delaying action: above all, time must be won. On May 18, the official demand for evacuation made by Egypt reached New York. The Consultative Committee of the UNEF (United Nations Expeditionary Force) rallied to the view of the Indian and Yugoslav representatives, whereas the Canadian representative, supported by the Danish one, vainly suggested once again that the problem should be laid before the Security Council.

Such are the facts: the Egyptians had created a *fait accompli*. In New York, the countries most directly implicated, India and Yugoslavia, because of their links with the United Arab Republic, pressed the Secretary-General to give the order for the evacuation. Thus it was President Nasser's friends, Marshal Tito and Mrs Gandhi, who set the infernal machine in motion that was to devastate the region. The clear-sightedness of the Canadians would have been of more service to the cause of peace and even to that of the United Arab Republic.

In spite of everything, U Thant would probably have gained a day or two if he had summoned the Security Council before ordering the evacuation. The Council would inevitably have been paralysed by the disagreement between the Great Powers, with the Soviet Union arguing for the Egyptian cause, which could hardly be contested from the legal point of view. While the Council was at its deliberations, would the President of the United States have succeeded in dissuading President Nasser from his fatal decision, the closure of the Straits of Tiran?

President Johnson was afraid above all else of a second Vietnam. In theory, he could and should have reminded President Nasser of the solemn commitments contracted by the United States government in 1957, at the time when Israeli troops evacuated Sharm-el-Sheik. He could and should have made him realize the gravity of a decision which had suddenly undermined the precarious equilibrium of the past ten years. In the actual circumstances of May 1967 the American President was beaten by the speed of events.

On May 22, President Nasser announced the blockade of the Straits of Tiran. At the end of the month, the problem of Aqaba had been overtaken in its turn: the pact between Jordan and the United Arab Republic and the entry of Iraqi troops into Jordan, were two more *casus belli* to be added to the first.

The crisis, and Arab propaganda left us in no doubt about this, challenged the very existence of the State of Israel.

What remains for us to find out? When and why President Nasser, after several years of caution, decreed the blockade of the Gulf of Aqaba, thereby defying not only Israel but also the

United States and Great Britain. From May 22 onwards, as after the Austrian ultimatum to Serbia in July 1914, the diplomatic crisis developed in accordance with the merciless logic of power politics: threats and counter-threats, an escalation of security measures and an upping of the stakes, a mobilization without war.

Even today, it remains surprising that the Israeli attack should have enjoyed the effect of surprise, when on May 26, Mr Mohammed Hasanein Haikal, a friend of President Nasser, had written: 'So it is no longer a question of the Gulf of Aqaba but of something more important: Israel's philosophy of security. That is why I say that Israel must attack.'

The UN and the Middle East Crisis:[1]

The Diplomacy of Loser Take All

The West has criticized U Thant for not having prevented a war won by the Israelis. In spite of the Arab defeat the Russians have not criticized him. Nasser's Yugoslav and Indian friends upheld the arguments of the President of the United Arab Republic in the corridors of the United Nations, while the representatives of neutral States, those of Canada and Denmark, were striving to defuse the bomb. Must we say, yet once more: beware of your friends?

There is no cause for astonishment that the preferences of Marshal Tito or Mrs Gandhi should have been displayed at the United Nations. This organization brings together sovereign States who frequently show signs of the partiality, cynicism even, characteristic of the 'cold-blooded monsters'. What remains not inexplicable but mysterious is that the Soviet Union, India and Yugoslavia did not foresee, as the Canadian diplomats did, the sequence of events from the closing of the Gulf of Aqaba to the Israeli attack on June 5. For the blockade of the Straits of Tiran made at least probable a war which the Indian government, which claims to be pacifist, should have used every means of preventing, and of which the government in Moscow, determined not to intervene directly in the event of hostilities, ought also to have been afraid.

Where did the leaders in the Kremlin go wrong? Over the dynamic of the conflict or the balance of strength? I don't know. The facts remain: Soviet diplomacy, after having apparently urged President Nasser on to a show of strength in order to

[1] October 27, 1967.

dissuade Israel from a punitive action against Syria, lost control of events. It became the prisoner of its own protégé, whom it could not or would not stop. Prior to June 5, it lent President Nasser unreserved verbal and moral support; on the morning of June 5, the hot-line was in action, and Russians and Americans were exchanging in private assurances of neutrality. The next day, they went back to exchanging in public insults and invective. The Soviet delegates even made the mistake of delaying the cease-fire by demanding the prior withdrawal of the Israeli troops. It was two days before they resigned themselves to the unconditional cease-fire, once the Arab defeats had become apparent and had persuaded them that the delay was favouring the Israelis. Once more, on the Monday, President Nasser's friends acted against his best interests.

The present rules of the diplomatic game, the blending of ideological propaganda with a limited and secret entente between the Big Two, make the conduct of all the participants, both big and small, intelligible. But if one stands back a bit, the impression of absurdity prevails. The same Soviet leaders who *could* not disown President Nasser when he created the *casus belli would* not take the slightest risk when the moment of truth came.

The same Yugoslav and Indian leaders, whose sympathies lay with the Arabs, lacked the clear-sightedness or the courage to intervene when the language of arms had still not drowned that of reason. Perhaps States always act out of self-interest, certainly they are not always good judges of that interest.

In May 1967, Marshal Tito would have helped the United Arab Republic if he had advised the Secretary-General of the United Nations not to withdraw the UN force immediately and persuaded President Nasser not to take the fatal decision to blockade the Straits of Tiran. But having, in the spring, shown the same blindness or ignorance as the other actors, he assumed in the summer a new role, a comic rather than a dramatic one. Without having talked to the statesmen of Israel he was going to re-establish peace in the Middle East.

* * *

At the United Nations, the same comedy that precipitated the explosion will be played out once again. The representatives of several dozen States will argue in favour of the Arab case without asking themselves about the means of taking effective action. Only the conversations in the wings will exert any appreciable influence.

The Russians have shown themselves more impatient than the Americans to reach a settlement that would enable the Suez Canal (used by the cargo ships going to North Vietnam) to be reopened, but they cannot force the Egyptian President to give in nor persuade the Americans to force the Israelis to make concessions. Apart from them, the only people to have been hit hard by the closure of the Canal are the Egyptians and the British. Now, the Israelis, despite threats of terrorism, want this time to obtain not an armistice but peace. And peace presupposes, apart from direct negotiations between Israel and her neighbours' frontiers that are accepted by all and a long-term plan offering the Palestinian refugees a hope of life.

*   *   *

Everyone knows quite well that all these declarations, the slanging of Israel, the speeches on behalf of the Arab case, the demand for the unconditional return of the Israeli troops to the positions they occupied before June 5, belong to that pseudo-diplomacy which unfolds in the world's pseudo-parliament. What is going to happen in the wings of the stage? Between May 16 and June 5, 1967, the friends of the Arabs were playing at loser take all. They created a situation in which the Israelis took the initiative in the hostilities and benefited from popular support even in those countries whose governments had denounced them as aggressors. Today, who is serving Israel's true and lasting interests the better, those working to maintain the *status quo* or those in the shadows preparing at least a temporary settlement?

In so far as we can forecast the future, the Arab States will not attempt a fourth trial of strength in the style and with the weapons of 1948, 1956 and 1967; tanks, aircraft, the desert, modern weapons and battlefields ensure a decisive advantage to the State that has a modern civilization. It hardly matters whether the border between Israel and Jordan runs along the River Jordan or not. The danger to the future existence of Israel comes from the Arab minority within the State, a minority that cannot be assimilated and may tomorrow be in revolt.

Israel cannot withhold citizenship from the Arabs without betraying her principles, she cannot grant it to them without compromising her very existence as a Hebrew nation: this contradiction will become all the more distressing as the Arab minority grows in numbers. Will the Israelis and their friends also play loser take all?

Part 3
Before the Crisis

The Jews[1]

Must we speak of it? A few weeks ago, as if by a wave from a magic wand, swastikas suddenly appeared, drawn or painted on walls in the four corners of Europe: Jewish cemeteries and synagogues were defiled. In answer, there was a growing number of indignant protests, from government leaders, from the press and from bodies dedicated to the fight against racialism. But the incidents soon vanished into oblivion and the sultry silence of guilty consciences reigned once more.

It has become almost as hard for a Jew as for a non-Jew to speak his mind. A Jew who is a non-believer and, in a way, 'de-judaized', risks offending those of his 'co-religionists' who have remained faithful to the Law. If he is a non-Zionist he is suspected alternately of having too much or too little sympathy for Israel. As for the non-Jews, they are inhibited by the extermination of six million Jews by Hitler. The event itself, the organizing of the slaughter of millions of defenceless beings into an industry, has afflicted people's consciences with a sort of trauma. Every man of breeding denies deep down having had the slightest responsibility in this monstrosity. No one dare admit either to others or to himself that he is a 'parlour' anti-semite. Even Maurras's disciples no longer expound their mentor's doctrines without a certain reticence. Both Jews and non-Jews repress memories too charged with emotion and find freedom in forgetfulness.

It is not my ambition to deal in a few pages with both the past and the present of the Jews and the anti-semites. I simply want, as a committed sociologist, to fix my bearings in the present situation. I say 'committed sociologist', and I value these two words. As teacher, journalist or writer I belong with those who

[1] Published in *Réalités*, September 1960.

do not like 'I', and who use it as little as possible. My life and innermost thoughts are of no concern to anyone else; I feel myself accountable for what I teach or write, and for the facts I observe or the ideas I defend. The private sphere lies hidden on either side of them. But when it comes to the Jews and to their destiny it would be hypocritical of me to pretend to the objectivity of the mere spectator. Better to confess right away who I am. My readers will then know enough to judge whether or not the commitment of the man has falsified the perspectives of the sociologist.

I belong to a Jewish family that came from Lorraine, but my parents were no longer either practising Jews or believers. I received hardly any religious instruction, and I could count on the fingers of my hand the number of times I was taken to church in my childhood. The culture I was given was French and bore no visible marks of the Jewish tradition. Moreover, for me Christianity was *the* religion, the one which the philosophers I read so passionately had revealed to me, the one I referred to in order to define the rights and demands of reason. I belong, therefore, with those Jews whom Sartre, in his essay, holds to be typical: they are Jews because the outside world declares them to be so, they assume their Jewishness out of dignity, but they do not feel it spontaneously.

But let us consider further. In so far as I have left the Jewish community and feel myself to be 'a Frenchman like the rest', without any links with my 'co-religionists', I could take exception to the judgment whereby my social milieu decrees that I am a Jew. I would be wrong, for the community to which my grandparents still belonged remains close at hand. What is the nature of this community? That will be a matter for debate, but I have to recognize that I am of 'Jewish origin' even though I refuse to say 'Jewish by religion'. It goes without saying that, as from 1933 and the rise to power of Hitler, a Jew, even one wholly detached from the faith of his fathers could not but claim openly an affiliation which was, in the event, to entail a certain danger.

As an 'assimilated' or 'de-judaized' Jew, to revert to those common expressions, I do not exclude theological interpretations of the destiny of the Jews, but nor do I subscribe to them.

This destiny seems to me to be no more inexplicable in terms of history than that of any other people. What is the point of invoking the wrath or the mercy of God in order to understand the survival of a group fiercely attached to its one God and its Law, or the persecutions endured by those who would not admit the divinity of Christ? Theological interpretations do not replace historical ones, they are located on a plane to which reason has no access.

But it is the duty of theology not to invent facts in order to make its case. The diaspora preceded the coming of Christ and cannot be shown as a divine sanction on the attitude adopted by the Jews (which Jews?) towards the man whom Christians love as the Son of God. No more does the destruction of the temple by Titus mark the end of the Jewish community in Palestine.

Again, Christians, inevitably, even those like Jacques Maritain who feel most sympathy for the Jews, give a meaning, in the sacred story, to the sufferings of the chosen people, but the sociologist cannot deny himself a few morose reflections. If the sufferings of the Jews have been willed from on high, are men not going to experience the temptation to cooperate in the fulfilment of the divine will (just as the Marxists help readily in the realization of the law of history)?

Neither a race nor a people

Who are the Blochs, the Isaacs, the Cohens, Levys or Arons whose names identify them and who know they are Jews because they have learned the unique story of their ancestors, the unique story of those who are called alternately a race and a people but who, in the strict sense of the term, form neither a race nor a people?

The Jews are not a race. Those anthropologists who measure skulls, analyse blood-groups and stick to physical characteristics that can be objectively detected, are almost unanimous on this point. The Jews scattered throughout the world display no homogeneity. What is more, one only needs to have been in Israel to confirm that Jews from Iraq look much more like Iraqi Muslims than Jews from Russia or France. In Beersheba I met a group of Jews from India who were indistinguishable from

Hindu Indians. No one could have confused them with the old
believers in the villages of Poland with their *payoths*, or the sturdy
fellows, with broad thighs, blond hair and blue eyes, who I had
seen in the kibbutzim on the borders driving tractors or handling
machine-guns.

History confirms what present observation suggests. Today's
Jews are not, for the most part, descended from the Jews of
Palestine who, after the destruction of the Kingdom of Jerusalem, departed throughout the world. In the last centuries before
Christ and the early centuries of our own era, Jewish communities flourished around the rim of the Mediterranean basin, made
up of converts to Judaism as much as emigrants from Judea. In
the second and third centuries A.D., Judaism and Christianity
were both proselytizing religions, akin but in competition. The
Gallo-Romans who were converted to Judaism were no different
racially from the Gallo-Romans converted to Christianity. And
for myself I do not think that Léon Poliakof's witticism was
wrong, however startling it may seem to some. His almost
legendary formula, 'our forefathers the Gauls', has just as good
a chance of applying to young French Jews as to their Christian
comrades. The Jews are of European and not Semitic stock.

Neither are the Jews 'a people like the rest', because, for nearly
two thousand years, between the destruction of the Kingdom of
Jerusalem and the creation of Israel, they were not organized
politically, they did not create a State. Yet, in spite of the diversity
of the fates they underwent at the hands of those around them,
they never fused with the populations they were living among.
The term that is used of 'Jewish community', suggests their un-
common destiny: the Jews had their own religion, faith, customs,
sometimes their own language (Yiddish) and culture. They were
a people without a State and faithful to a religion that ordered
the whole of their lives, and they were, by turns, persecuted and
respected, tolerated and expelled. At one moment, they would be
made welcome and seemed to be about to lose their peculiarities
and merge with the Gentiles, at the next, rejected by the world
around them, they developed their unique style of life and beliefs
in the ghetto.

The situation of the Jews has varied with the centuries and
with civilizations. Take their situation simply in the Christian

world. Without trying to settle the controversy that still divides historians over whether anti-semitism existed before Christ, how can it be denied that the Jewish question, such as it has been posed in Europe in modern times, derives from an anti-semitism that has developed inside a civilization steeped in Christianity?

In one sense Christians ought not to be anti-semitic, in another sense they are prone to be so. Christ was born a Hebrew. Religiously speaking, as the Popes have proclaimed, Christians are Semites, and anti-semitism, which is based on a racialist concept that holds the Jewish people to be biologically inferior, is incompatible with adhesion to a Christian church. But, in another sense, the Jews have remained faithful to the Old Testament and not recognized the Messiah whose coming was heralded by the prophets. What is more, they put him to death. Thus the Jewish people, from which Christ came, has become the people of deicides, and the misfortunes that have overwhelmed them, the destruction of the temple and the diaspora, have been interpreted by many learned Christian scholars as a divine punishment for their inexpiable crime.

Historians deny the responsibility of the Jewish people for the Crucifixion. Read, in this connection, Jules Isaac's *Jésus et Israël*, and ponder some of the propositions that historian has tried to prove: 'The Gospels are evidence that wherever Jesus went, with very few exceptions, the Jewish people gave him an enthusiastic welcome . . . We do not have the right to assert that the Jewish people rejected Christ or the Messiah, or that it rejected the Son of God, before it has been proven that Jesus revealed himself as such to the Jewish people as a whole and that he was rejected by that people as a whole . . . It is claimed that Christ passed sentence on the Jewish people and condemned them to their downfall. But why would he have given the lie to his Gospel of forgiveness and love and condemned his own people, the one people he chose to address, the people among whom he had found, along with zealous enemies, fervent disciples and adoring crowds? There is every reason to believe that what was truly condemned was the real culprit, a certain Pharisaism that can be found in all times and in all peoples, in all religions and in all Churches . . .' And I would like to remind you of a sentence quoted by Jules Isaac from Charles Péguy: 'It was not the Jews who crucified Jesus Christ, but the sins of all of us; and the Jews who were only the instrument share like everyone else in the fountain-head of salvation.'

I know very well that many theologians and Christian historians would dispute Jules Isaac's propositions, and that even in the eyes of a Christian who subscribed to all of them it would remain true that 'believing' Jews are 'unbelievers' who deny the divinity of Christ. Even were the 'inculcation of contempt' to vanish, Christians and Jews would still be opposed as believers, since the latter reject the New Testament which the former see as fulfilling the promise of the Old.

What does this theological and historical quarrel have in common with the present Jewish question? the sceptical reader will ask. Hitler felt the same hatred for Jews and Christians alike. If he had won the war he would, after exterminating the Jews, have taken up the struggle against the Christians, in particular the Catholic Church. The small shopkeeper who execrated the Jews because he confused them with the owners of the big stores knew nothing about the Passion or the people of deicides. I am not disregarding the gap, both psychological and historical, between the rivalry of Judaism and Christianity at the end of the Roman Empire, and the social conflicts of today. But if we neglect this religious opposition, we cannot grasp why and how the Jews have become, over the centuries, the scapegoats of Christian societies, responsible for all their misfortunes and the appointed target of their desire for revenge and expiation. The first pogroms of which there is a record took place in the year 1096, a few months after Pope Urban II had preached the First Crusade at the Council of Clermont-Ferrand. In this instance, it is impossible to doubt the religious origin of anti-semitism. If the Crusades, fired by the love of Christ, put to death Jewish men, women and children who would not consent to being baptized, it was not out of resentment or a liking for pillage. They were going to fight the enemies of God in the East: how could they have spared 'a race that was more the enemy of God than any other'? Already, at the time of the bloodiest and most systematic massacres, those of Speyer, Worms and Mainz, the Jews had sought and often obtained the protection of bishops against

Crusades which believed they were acting as Christians when they turned themselves into the instruments of God's wrath against the people of outcasts.

Religious rivalry was the cause of the strange fate afflicting the Jews through the centuries. This strange fate in turn left its mark on Jewish communities and on the way in which Jews lived and thought. The Jews remained stubbornly faithful to their Law, especially when the society around them condemned or despised them; they were intransigent monotheists, convinced of the pact between God and His people, members of a nation yet universalist, unable because of their faith and, even more, of Christian reaction to that faith, to lose their identity, the source both of their pride and their misfortune.

It is from these initial facts that the dialectic of the 'Jewish situation' and the 'Jewish character' has developed, which pro-Semites and anti-Semites still comment on purely in terms of opposition. The Jews of the urban communities, the Jews of the ghetto, the Jews who are forbidden to own land or follow the profession of arms, cannot but display some social and psychological characteristics that mark them off from the Gentiles. But are they what they are, anxious, critical, bitter, money-grubbing tradesmen, thirsters after the absolute, revolutionaries, musicians and who knows what else, because of the condition imposed on them over so many centuries, or because their heredity itself predisposes them to certain activities, endows them with certain qualities and saddles them with certain faults?

We shall halt for a while over this question, to which, obviously, there is no categorical answer. But, for all that, it is not impossible to indicate certain indisputable facts.

Between the great banker or the Jew at court and the Rabbi or the itinerant vendor, there was almost as wide a gap as between poor man and rich man, peasant and nobleman, in Christian societies. Can one ascertain characteristics common both to court Jews and village rabbis, to the Jew from Iraq and the Jew from Avignon, which might provide some sort of basis for a popular image of the Jewish character and the unique essence of the Jewish people? Perhaps these common characteristics do exist elsewhere than in our own imaginations. At all events, there are several circumstances that enable us to give an account of them without penetrating the mystery of history or believing in miracles.

The Jews have owed their coherence and their capacity for survival both to the intransigence of their faith in a single God and to the intermittent hostility and constant opposition of the world around them. The culture of the Jewish communities has been profoundly influenced by that of the nations among whom they were living, but their reading of the Bible, the work of the Talmudists and the intellectual formation attributable to beliefs and tradition, left their mark on Jewish minds. Afterwards, what had been brought into being and preserved by many different circumstances was ascribed to the genius of a people.

But I must not go too far in this direction : perhaps hereditary gifts are not distributed evenly throughout the human species. Jews, say some, have a gift for metaphysical speculation, mathematics and trade, they do not have a gift for the profession of arms, agriculture or creative intuition. Obviously, they do not mean that all Jews possess or lack these gifts; they mean, or ought to mean, that the number of those gifted or not gifted for this or that is proportionately higher amongst Jews than amongst non-Jews. Such a hypothesis is hard to prove, and if it is not dictated by the facts neither is it contradicted by them. If we were to assume that the so-called Jewish propensities are partly hereditary, the visible expression of this heredity owes a lot to the social conditions under which the Jews have lived, and to the ideas and customs that have arisen and have crystallized through the centuries. Having become fully-fledged citizens, just like the rest, to what extent do they lose the peculiarities from which they sometimes derive pride and which non-Jews lay alternately to their credit and their debit?

Which brings us to the present situation. At the end of a historical experiment of more or less total liberation, which had lasted about a century for Europe as a whole but significantly less in the Eastern half of the Old Continent, Hitler's fury fell on all Jews, orthodox and unbelievers, those loyal to the faith of their fathers and those completely detached from it. In 1945, there remained fewer than 100,000 Jews out of three and a half million who had been living in Poland before the war. In Germany, there were some 800,000 when Hitler came to power, many of whom emigrated before 1939. Today they number some 20,000 to 30,000 in the Federal Republic. The Jewish communities established in Holland, which had become an integral part of the nation without losing their originality, were completely wiped out. About a third of the Jews who found themselves in France in 1940 perished.

Eastern and Western attitudes to Israel

Following the Jewish emigration to Palestine and the events which led to the ending of the British mandate, the State of Israel was created in 1948. Henceforth world Judaism had three centres: Israel, an independent State, permanently open in principle to all the Jews of the diaspora wanting to settle in the Holy Land; the United States with its some five million Jews; and the Soviet Union with some three million.

At the present time, a Jew has to define himself by adopting a position on two issues: his religion and its traditions, and Israel. For the existence of Israel, far from resolving the Jewish problem, in so far as that problem has a solution, has given it an extra dimension.

In actual fact, a Frenchman of the Jewish faith has a right to full and complete French citizenship while still remaining faithful to the synagogue. Each of us has a country *and* a religion, but *no one can have two countries*. The Jew who feels that his political loyalty is to Israel is under an obligation to match his actions to his feelings, that is to emigrate to the Holy Land. I want this to be understood: it is normal and probably inevitable that most Jews should have sympathy, admiration and respect for the work of their co-religionists in Israel. It would be surprising and even, truth to tell, somewhat shocking, if they did not. I feel very remote from those European Jews (and there are some) who criticize Israel, perhaps unconsciously, for having supplied a fresh argument to possible persecutors in the future.[1]

But I feel equally remote from those Jews in Europe who do not want to become citizens of Israel but who yet feel themselves bound to take the Israeli side under all circumstances. Since, during the past few years, France has been in almost permanent

[1] There is no great merit in having made this prediction (1967).

5

conflict with the world of Islam, this double loyalty, to France and to Israel, has not created any problems of conscience. A French journalist of Jewish origin whom I know well and who was opposed to the Sinai campaign and the Ango-French expedition to Suez, found himself being upbraided for his attitude by the management of his paper: what, you, a Jew, leave the job of justifying Israel to us! I had to answer that citizenship cannot be divided. I do not feel bound to approve Israeli diplomacy whatever decisions it takes.

On the other hand, it seems legitimate to me that the Frenchman of Jewish origin should claim the right to stick to his faith and those elements of his traditional culture to which he is attached. Why should a Jew have to give up, by assimilation, the beliefs and practices of his fathers, in order to be a good Frenchman or a good Englishman? Only the avowed or shamefaced dogmatists of totalitarianism demand such an alienation as the price of citizenship. In the Soviet Union, as we shall see, the condition of Jew seems in itself to be an aggression against the State. There is nothing of that sort in the democratic societies of the West.

Moreover, during the liberal period, de-judaization was carried out more rapidly than the orthodox or even mere believers might have wished. In France, Germany, Austria and Hungary Jews took an active and often leading part in intellectual life, and in the creations of science and art. Their contribution was intended to be fully national, that is French in France, German in Germany. At the time of the first world war, the Jews of France felt themselves to be Frenchmen and the German Jews Germans, long before they felt their supposed Jewish solidarity. After 1933, I knew Jews who saw the émigrés fleeing from Hitler above all as Germans.

Personally, if I were asked what conclusion I draw from the 'experiment' of the liberal century, I would not hesitate: I draw the exactly opposite conclusion from the one most commonly held. The Jewish communities would not have resisted if the experiment had lasted. Not that a number of Jews might probably have not remained as practising Jews or believers, faithful to the Bible and expounding the Talmud. But most of them would have been won over by the spirit of rationalism and criticism.

They would have grown increasingly ignorant of the true Judaic tradition and less and less distinguishable from their compatriots, or at least from those of the same social position and profession as themselves (it is too easy to oppose Léon Blum to the peasants of Brittany or Picardy: was Barrès all that much like the peasants of Lorraine?). Jews can become 'Frenchmen like the rest' or 'Germans like the rest', in the same way as, collectively, they are becoming, in Israel, 'a nation like the rest'.

Israel is a democratic State and a secular nation.[1] Both State and nation were created by men who, for the most part, believed more in the Bible than in God. The first generation of pioneers in Israel, who had come from Russia and from Poland, reacted against the anti-semitism of their environment in the manner of modern nationalists and not, to use the concept of the English historian Arnold Toynbee, as remote descendants of Syrian civilizations. They aspired to a country of their own because the people they were living amongst had refused them possession of the country most of them aspired to, that of the land they were living on and the language they were speaking.

Israel, a non-theocratic State bound together by religion, an apparently religious State whose founders did not all believe in God, remains a permanent paradox. Does it mark a stage in the sacred history, the reconstruction of the Temple, the proof that God does not desert his people and that the prophecy is being fulfilled? For the most part, the orthodox do not exactly know what meaning to give the State of Israel, since it is an episode in profane history and does not herald, with the return to Jerusalem, the end of history or the salvation of a finally united mankind. Thus some of them show a certain reticence towards Israel because they are concerned for the spiritual destiny of Judaism and fear that a faith which they see as sublime may be degraded into a political fanaticism.

But with these doubts are mixed other human, or too human feelings. Having been so often accused of being unable to fight (in the first centuries A.D., before Constantine's conversion to Christianity, large numbers of them served in the Roman legions!) the Jews can but derive some pride from the

---

[1] This formula is not wholly accurate. In Israel an Israeli man cannot marry a non-Jew (1967).

military feats of the Israeli army. An Israeli diplomat of French origin, whom I spoke to in Jerusalem about the old believers' attitude towards the young State, recounted to me an episode he had witnessed during the war of liberation. The *payath* Jews, who belonged to a group previously opposed to the creation of the State, could not help, when they saw the first tank bearing the rosette decorated with the Star of David, weeping and shouting with joy. Thus, all over the world, the Talmudists are hesitating between spiritual refusal and quasi-national enthusiasm.

For the present, the creation of Israel has not noticeably altered the situation of the Jews in Western Europe and the United States. In French minds Israel awoke sympathies that have sometimes erred over Frenchmen of Jewish origin. The memory of the Final Solution has repressed the open expression of a hostility whose possible and tragic outcome has been shown by events. There was no comparable reaction when M. René Mayer or M. Mendès-France became President of the Council to the one unleashed in 1936 by the presidency of Léon Blum. The unpopularity which does not usually spare the associates of a great man has fallen on M. Michel Debré, but he is not criticized (in fact hardly anyone knows it) for being the grandson of a rabbi.

In the United States, the Jews, the majority of them favourable to Israel, have displayed their sympathy by generously subscribing each year millions of dollars. A minority has shown itself reluctant or hostile, either out of religious traditionalism or from fear of the repercussions which the existence of the Israeli State might have on the Jews of the diaspora. An even smaller minority has given up its American citizenship in order to emigrate to the Holy Land.

Beyond the Iron Curtain, on the other hand, Israel and Zionism have become terms of contempt. Every day Israel is denounced as an outpost of American imperialism, although in 1948 the Soviet Union was quick to recognize the new State. Zionism as such passes for reactionary, as a form of cosmopolitanism or, at the opposite extreme, of bourgeois nationalism. In keeping with the early teachings of Bolshevism and of all the Socialist schools (the formula has not been forgotten that was freely repeated in Socialist circles at the start of the century: 'anti-semitism is the poor man's Socialism'), anti-semitism is still banned; in conversation with Westerners the Soviet leaders have declared vigorously that they loathed anti-semitism and had combated it. In connection with the Doctors' murder trial, Mr Khrushchev himself declared: 'The whole affair has been given a Jewish Zionist tinge. That was engineered by Beria. As Zionists they were accused of being American spies, after earlier being accused of medical sabotage against Zhdanov and others. That was ridiculous. It wasn't a Jew who attended Zhdanov anyway, it was Doctor Yegorov.' And, in connection with Israel, Mr Khrushchev said: 'We are not in favour of travelling to Israel . . . We are against it because Israel is under the thumb of the American reactionaries. Consequently all spying and provocation can easily be channelled through Israel. It is the aftermath of the cold war that dictates our particular attitude towards Israel. We hope that this will be temporary and that this attitude will pass.'

Three elements in the Soviet policy can be isolated from these remarks: an official condemnation of anti-semitism, an official assertion of anti-Zionism and of hostility towards Israel, an avowal of the 'anti-Jewish' tone given by Beria to the trials during the closing stages of Stalinism. What are the facts of the matter?

One initial fact is no longer denied today by anybody: between 1948 and 1953 the Jews in the Soviet Union were persecuted because they were Jews, although in the language of the authorities the word used may have been Zionist.

During the final years of Stalin's life, 'tens of thousands of Jews were removed from their jobs, arrested or interned . . . the wave of persecution reached its height after the secret trial of August 1952 in the arrest of the Kremlin doctors. The Doctors' trial fixed for March 13, 1953 was to have furnished a justification for the massive deportation of Jews to Siberia and the Arctic regions planned by Stalin'. (F. Fejtö: *Les Juifs et l'anti-sémitisme dans les pays communistes.*') According to Léon Leneman (*La Tragédie des Juifs en U.R.S.S.*) Ilya Ehrenburg would have crowned a cynical and sinister career by giving evidence at the trial against the élite of the Jewish intelligentsia.

Today the Jews are no longer exposed to such perils. According to witnesses, they seem to enjoy physical security. But they do not for all that feel that they are treated on an equal footing.

The crisis originates in the unique destiny of Judaism, which is neither a religion like the rest nor a nationality like the rest. I appeal here to a writer who cannot be suspected of hostility towards the Soviet Union, Professor Hyman Levy, an English mathematician who has adhered strictly to the party line for many years and who has written a little book called *Jews and the National Question*. In the Soviet Union, all citizens belong to a nationality which is noted on their passports. Jews, whether they live in Moscow or Kiev, in Kharkov or Tiflis, in North, South, East or West, are designated as Jews and not as Russians or Ukrainians, Belorussians or Georgians. In the Soviet Union, therefore, the Jews constitute a nationality that is 'not like the rest' since it is scattered throughout other nationalities and has no territorial base.

The Soviet leaders thought up, with more or less seriousness, a territorial solution that was to be the equivalent in the Socialist world of Israel in the Western world: the autonomous region of Birobidzhan. The experiment miscarried. The autonomous region of Birobidzhan hardly counts in the destiny of Soviet Jewry.

There remains the essential contradiction. As a scattered nationality without a territorial base, the Jews do not get the same rights freely to develop their own culture and language as other nationalities.

The Soviet authorities claim that the Jews themselves have no more use for their traditions. But such declarations are hardly borne out by the evidence, by the spontaneous demonstrations around the Israeli Embassy, by official propaganda against Zionism and bourgeois nationalism. The Jews of the Soviet Union complain today of the restrictions imposed on their culture as well as the discrimination practised against them in all the republics; everywhere, in one way or another, they are aliens. This discrimination, and the subtle practice of the *numerus clausus*, varies with different professions, circumstances and moments. There is no doubt at all that it was provoked by numerous Jews in the Soviet Union becoming aware of their Jewishness once again. Where they were free to emigrate, a number of them left for Israel (the percentages advanced in various quarters, 20 per cent for example, are obviously pure speculation).

For my own part I cannot be astonished that the Soviet regime should display hostility towards the Jews despite the role they played in the movement of ideas and of the Socialist parties. A totalitarian State that sets out to embrace life in its entirety and subject it to an ideological discipline, thereby condemns itself to fight against this odd minority which will not abjure its faith and which remains linked to its 'co-religionists' beyond the frontiers. In a totalitarian State, until such time as they melt into the mass, the Jews represent an alien element because they are cosmopolitan.

On anti-semitism

Before the war, there were nearly five million Jews in Bulgaria, Czechoslovakia, Hungary, Poland and Romania; immediately after the war there were only about 680,000, and in 1957 some 375,000. The survivors in Eastern Europe are irremediably divided: some are Zionists and candidates for emigration to Israel (almost all Bulgaria's Jews emigrated to Israel immediately after the war), others are fervent Communists, aspiring to total 'de-judaization' and unconditional assimilation; others still would like to remain Jews yet not to go on being discriminated against in the country that is their own. In Poland and Hungary alike some of the fiercest and most abject Stalinists were Jews. Others, especially in Hungary, were amongst the leading revolutionists and revolutionaries in 1956. Popular anti-semitism has remembered above all the role of a few Jews in the excesses of Stalinism. In spite of the efforts of the regime, there was in Poland, after 1956, a recrudescence of anti-semitism.

Perhaps the reader is going to break in at this point: but what is this anti-semitism which you are discussing by implication in this article without ever defining it? I will answer indirectly in the first instance: a negative judgment on this or that intellectual or moral trait of the Jews is not in itself enough to define the anti-semite. I open, for example, André Siegfried's little book, *La Voie d'Israël* and I read:

The Jew is also a pessimist, conspicuously so in respect of the societies in which his destiny has caused him to live. As the result of intellectual disassociation he is able to judge this destiny with the cold lucidity of an outsider. Here I would recall a well-known passage by Barrès on Pico della Mirandola: 'Jewish intellects have a common denominator which anyone can detect in the interesting Israelites among his associates. They handle ideas the way a banker handles securities. Ideas do not seem, as is ordinarily the case, the formula in which they signify their appetites and the most intimate movements of their being, but counters which they sort out on a cold slab of marble.' We have already noted, indeed, that the Jew who criticizes the society he lives in does not criticize it as he might his mother, but with a certain mercilessness and ruthlessness. In spite of so many appearances to the contrary, he is almost never a conservative traditionalist, but much rather, in actual fact a revolutionary. If he is a conservative it is in his own tradition, and then he is so with passion and no longer over the cold marble of commercial exchange.

Can it be said that Bergson or Simone Weil, Freud or Einstein, handled ideas the way a banker handles securities? Must Disraeli be excluded either from conservatism or Judaism? Yet for all that, no one will accuse André Siegfried of anti-semitism. It is legitimate to draw up 'a moral portrait of the Jew', in spite of the dangers of such doubtful psychology when it sinks to the level of vulgarization. Inevitably, the portrait will include unattractive features (more or less numerous and more or less unattractive according to the leanings of the painter).

Nor shall I label as anti-semitic those authors, sometimes Jews, like Toynbee or Simone Weil, who interpret the essence of the Jewish people, religion or culture in their own way. According to Arnold Toynbee, the Jews are fossils of the civilization of Syria and have apparently created nothing for the last two thousand years or so; they are also the originators of political and religious fanaticism. In the same way, Simone Weil put the Jews on the wrong side of the barricade, on the side of the Roman conquerors, of *raison d'état* and totalitarianism, whereas the Greeks and Jesus are placed on the side of charity and salvation through grace: on the side of the pure. And F. Fejtö, himself a disillusioned Communist, writes: 'Where they are narrowminded and stubborn, and incapable of adhering in actuality to a supranational idea, all our modern forms of nationalism are "Jewish".' And Fejtö adds that 'the Jews are also the 'extremists' of Christianity . . . Their hands are empty, they believe in nothing, nothing at all. They are sucked in, as it were, by the absolute.' I must admit in all humility that I am not very taken with either this excess of honour or this indignity. Mankind has no need of the Jews in order to discover political or religious fanaticism nor to feel within itself an unslakable thirst for the absolute.

For my own part, I can see three sorts of anti-semite, whom I shall call 'religious', 'political' and 'affective'. Jules Isaac, rightly in my view, saw in religious anti-semitism, that which denounces the people of deicides, the origin of all the others. Christians have helped to propagate it because, in their eyes, the Jews are unbelievers; they did not recognize Christ and continue to adhere to the Law, although for the past two thousand years this has been saved and superseded by the Gospels.

'Political' anti-semitism is the one which refuses Jews equal status as citizens, and a full and complete share in the rights and obligations of citizenship. Maurras's State anti-semitism belonged in this category. Maurras would neither have ordered nor approved the mass executions of Jews,[1] but, according to his teachings, he would have established a *numerus clausus*, forbidding Jews to exercise certain professions or to succeed to certain positions.

This political anti-semitism invokes various arguments which all come back to the 'otherness' of Jewish life in relation to the national life (French or German). Maurras, who was not a racialist, saw the Jews as always representing an alien element in the body of the nation. Some hold that assimilation of the Jews *qua* Jews is still insufficient but not ultimately impossible, others hold it to to be excluded once and for all; some denounce their cosmopolitanism, others their alien nationalism, others again their meanness, innate or acquired.

With these last we come to 'affective' anti-semitism; hatred or contempt felt towards the Jews as a collectivity. It goes without saying that such feelings may be determined by the most varied

---

[1] Although, under the occupation, Maurras pointed out Jews to the German prosecutors (1967).

5*

causes. It is possible to study in each particular case the circumstances in which the 'affective' anti-semitism of this or that individual or group has originated, but such a study only touches on the external conditions of an 'existential' choice, it only encompasses the last stage of an age-old phenomenon: the exclusion from the common lot of communities that have not remained merely religious ones and which are not organized politically.

The racialism of Hitler partook of all three of these categories. But a biological philosophy turned hatred into a murdering fury. It was not enough for Hitler and his like to hound out the Jews, as the political anti-semites would have done, or to portray them in hideous colours as the affective anti-semites do, they needed to exterminate them as a noxious species, not because they had crucified the Messiah but perhaps because Christ had come from their race.

To my mind, what I have written here does not contain a conclusion. I would be angry with myself if I fixed or claimed to have fixed the responsibility of either side in this tragic story. Everything has already been said and repeated ad infinitum about the contradictions of the Jewish consciousness, and the paradox of believers who love the God of all mankind yet maintain they are the chosen people. For my own part, I re-read Spinoza's *Tractatus Theologico-Politicus*; I believe 'that nations are different one from another, I mean in respect of their social system and of the laws under which they live and govern themselves', but that 'everyone, Gentile as much as Jew, has lived under the Law, by which I mean that which alone is concerned with true virtue, not that which is established in respect of each State'. More than ever I believe that 'in respect of understanding and of true virtue, no nation has been made any different from another, and so, in this respect, there is no nation which God has chosen in preference to others ... Today, therefore, there is absolutely nothing which the Jews can claim for themselves which would set them above all other nations.' Nothing, I would add, except misfortune, and nothing which would set them below other nations either.

I shall never be a militant in the anti-anti-semitic organizations. It is not for us Jews to boast about our virtues or denounce those who do not like us. As an individual, I claim the right to be a Frenchman without betraying my ancestors, to have a country without giving up my religion, even if, in point of fact, I no longer adhere to it. The rest does not depend on me, the rest does not depend on us.

At the conclusion of his essay on the Jewish question, Jean-Paul Sartre quotes the Negro writer Richard Wright, who said: 'There is no black problem in the United States, there is only a white problem.' Sartre adds: 'Similarly, we shall say that anti-semitism is not a Jewish problem, it is our problem.'

The Jews and the State of Israel

This article was prefaced, in the *Figaro Littéraire* for February 24, 1962, by the following foreword:

A few months ago, an American publisher asked me to write an essay for a compilation in honour of the memory of Chaim Weizmann, the first President of the Israeli Republic. I accepted, without hiding the fact that, whatever sympathy I had for the State of Israel, my personal views were far removed from those of the Zionists. Recently, the publisher informed me that the conception of the book had changed; all the essays would be concerned with the biography of the great man.

Pierre Brisson considered that this text might be of interest to the readers of the *Figaro Littéraire*: I hope that it will not give offence to any of my 'co-religionists'.

Now that there is once again a flourishing State of Israel is it possible to be a Jew away from the Promised Land? The question was raised, a few months ago, by Mr Ben Gurion. It has been passionately debated; those who maintain 'yes' and those who maintain 'no' have both borrowed quotations favourable to their respective cases freely from the wise men of the past. But, beyond the scholastic or Talmudic quarrels, there is one fact that cannot be doubted: the Jews of Babylon did not all go back to Palestine when, around 520 B.C., the Temple of Jerusalem, having been raised from its ruins, was dedicated to the worship of Jahveh. The Jews may, over the centuries, have dreamed of their lost homeland, they may, though with varying degrees of vigour, have aspired to return to it. It has never been a religious obligation for a Jew to live in Palestine or to become a citizen of the State which, more than two thousand years ago and since 1948, was rebuilt around Jerusalem.

It is not for me, who am not a believer in the usual sense of that word, to take part in this controversy. But, stripped of its biblical allusions, Mr Ben Gurion's question is addressed to all Jews. The State of Israel, as a secular State, wants to be like the other States of our own century, although it displays certain characteristics which make it unique. Must the French, English or American Jew feel attached to Israel as to his own country? If so, by what right could he claim the privileges of a citizen in France, Great Britain or the United States? Everyone may love his own country and his God, everyone can belong to both a religious community and a political entity. But no one can claim the right to a double citizenship. Modern citizenship involves, essentially, obedience to the commands of the State, and above all, to military obligations. I may be a Frenchman of the Jewish religion, I cannot be both French and Israeli. However much sympathy I may feel for Israel, I must not hide from myself the fact that no pre-established harmony exists between the national interests of France and those of Israel. If, in order to avoid a distressing conflict, I postulate *a priori* that the interests of these two countries are one, I am failing in my duty as a Frenchman, an Englishman or an American. For my duty as a citizen orders me not to assess 'the interest of my country' in terms of *one* exclusive consideration, or to subordinate it in advance to the interests of some other political entity. The self-centredness of nations is not sacred, but nations are, and are condemned to be, self-centred.

It is no good objecting that the interests of the country in which the diaspora has placed me cannot come into conflict with the interests of Israel because France, Great Britain or the United States would be failing in their vocation and would release me from my oath of loyalty if they fought against or merely deserted Israel. Such an objection is valueless, it involves a logical fallacy: relations between sovereign political entities are not subject either to laws or law-courts. There is no police force capable of disciplining rival and spontaneous wills to power. Every State aspires to survival and, in order to survive, must be ready if not to commit injustice then to allow injustice to be committed. As a political entity, France, with her limited resources and exposed to constant dangers, has no more obligations in respect of Israel than of any other State. I risk acting as a bad Frenchman if I use my influence to persuade my fellow-countrymen to judge Israel favourably *a priori*. This sort of speculation may appear futile or untimely, France and Israel having been, for better or for worse, linked by an unwritten pact for the past few years. But this situation may easily be reversed. When the State of Israel was first proclaimed, the French government hesitated first of all to recognize it, fearing the reactions of the Muslims in North Africa. The actual pact with Israel also resulted from the situation in North Africa. The Algerian conflict once past, it is not impossible to imagine concern for a reconciliation with the Muslim countries of North Africa turning France away from Israel.

What is the good, in any case, of insisting on what is self-evident? The day the Zionists decided to become Israelis, that is to create a national, secular-type State, they thereby broke with their 'co-religionists' who had neither the means nor the desire to join them in Palestine. The Israelis have declared implicitly at least that the Jewish community is, in its essence and vocation, national, whereas the Jews of the diaspora maintain that this community is religious or cultural in essence and has no national vocation in so far as the idea of a nation can be fulfilled only in and through independence as a State.

Agreed, the Jewish communities of the diaspora were divided before the State of Israel was founded. It would be absurd to charge it with being responsible for a break-up constituted by the diaspora itself. Between 1914 and 1918 the Jews of France and Germany did not cut themselves off from their adoptive countries, they faced each other on either side of the firing line, and fought without hesitation or remorse, 'Frenchmen and Germans just like the rest'. But it was exactly the same for Catholics and Protestants; they too killed one another, in the trenches of Verdun, even though their faith was directed at the same God of love and priests belonging to the same Church were ready to assist them in their last moments. But when French Jews fought German Jews they were fighting as French soldiers and German soldiers, never as Jewish soldiers. If the State of Israel were to find itself at war with a country that contained a Jewish minority, diaspora Jews would be fighting against Jews who were soldiers because they were Jews.

The only object of such an eventuality, luckily improbable in present conditions or in the foreseeable future, is to illustrate a possible rift or, if you prefer, an extreme situation and, at the same time, to pose the problem which any Jew, believer or not, whether conscious of his Judaism or 'de-judaized', must confront squarely. Who am I? What do I want to be in relation to Israel?

If I look around me, I observe four 'categories' or 'types' of Jew: (1) those who adhere in the main to their traditional faith; (2) those who, although they do not believe in the covenant between God and His people or even in God, are still wedded to Jewish traditions and culture and want to safeguard their originality; (3) those who have been 'assimilated' by their environment to the point of becoming completely detached from the Jewish community, whose culture they no longer know except from the outside; (4) finally, those who are or want to become Israelis and who, oddly enough, are recruited just as much among believers as among non-believers still wedded to tradition, or even among assimilated Jews (whenever they are disappointed or affected by some brutal outbreak of anti-semitism). The undeniable fact that not all the Jews who either aspire to or have obtained Israeli nationality are religious is unsurprising. When Zionism spread through Europe at the end of the last century, its inspiration was not religious but political.[1] It was the recoil from European nationalism. The founders of Zionism believed more in Judaism than in God. They did not justify a home for Jews or the Jewish State by the religious demand for the return to the Promised Land. It was not to embellish their prayers that they dreamed of Jerusalem. It was not the Temple that fired their imaginations but the State. European Jews wanted to provide themselves with a country. And since the Russians, the Poles and even the Germans and French refused to welcome them as fully-fledged citizens they would build a nation that would not treat them as intruders because it would be Jewish. Historically, it was European nationalism in the nineteenth century that led to the birth of Zionism

---

[1] This crude formula now asks at least to be qualified (1967).

and so, indirectly, to the State of Israel. Should this event be seen as a diverting of the course of Jewish history? Or as the fulfilment of an ancient promise and a permanent vocation?

*   *   *

Is the Jewish community an ethnic, a cultural, a religious or a national one? The answer inevitably reflects the complexity of the reality, the ambiguity of the concepts and the peculiarity of the Jewish experience.

Ethnically speaking, the unity of the Jews is at the very least imperfect. In all probability, the Jewish communities in India and China originated chiefly with the conversions of Indians and Chinese, not with the immigration of Jews from Palestine. Investigations carried out into the comparative frequency of blood groups in the various Jewish communities and in the populations surrounding them, do not lead to any indisputable conclusions, but they make it at least probable that the European Jews of today are not all descended from Palestinian Jews. During the first centuries after Christ in the West, and later in the East, both individuals and large groups were converted to the Jewish religion. Even if one were to admit that, thanks to the endogamy practised or imposed on them, most Jews today are descended from the Jews of Palestine, it would be inaccurate to talk of a race. The Jews do not constitute a distinct anthropological group, comparable with those which the scientists call a race. It is not excluded, though neither is it proven, that certain genes, leading to certain physical characteristics or certain psychological predispositions, may appear with a higher frequency among Jewish people than among others. Hereditary peculiarities, whose reality, once again, is still only a hypothesis, are not enough to constitute an ethnic entity, still less a consciousness of forming an ethnic entity. A European Jew is not conscious of forming an ethnic entity with a Yemeni Jew (even when both are citizens of the State of Israel).

On the other hand, Jews have constituted 'cultural and religious communities' which in several respects have no equivalent. In actual fact, these communities were all influenced, positively or negatively, by the world around them, by the culture of the society they were living in. Thus, all that these scattered communities had in common was religion (even then there were secondary variations in belief and especially in ritual). In relation to their environment, the Jewish communities constituted something that was over and above a religious community. In relation to each other, they had no other links but a faith, based on a Book and on commentaries on that Book. In the absence of a Church and an ecclesiastical hierarchy, the Jewish communities of the diaspora did not live the same history or have a conscious desire to be a nation.

Yet one cannot assert that over the centuries the Jews have remained alien to the idea of a nation. It is even possible to write a history of the Jewish people centred around 'the will of the Jews to maintain a national identity'. Thus, in the twelfth volume of *A Study of History* (page 483), Arnold Toynbee writes:

The Jews may be defined as being the conscious and deliberate heirs and representatives of the people of the Kingdom of Judah, which was extinguished by the Neobabylonian Emperor Nebuchadnezzar in the second decade of the sixth century B.C. Ever since that fearful national disaster the paramount aim of the Judaism deported to Babylon and their Jewish descendants has been to preserve unbroken their distinctive *national* identity [my italics] . . . This record is recognized, by friendly and hostile observers alike, as being an extraordinary monument of steadfastness or obstinacy – whichever of the two words the observer may feel inclined to use. The achievement has been possible only because the Jews have always consistently given priority over other aims of theirs to this aim of preserving their distinctive national identity.

This passage displays a typically smooth transition from a factual proposition that cannot be contested to an interpretation of it which is, at the very least, controversial. There can be no doubt that the Jews have preserved their 'identity' over the past 2,500 years. That they should have sought to maintain it is a very probable inference, since non-assimilation over such a long period could not be exclusively explained by a rejection (which has not been a constant one) of the world around them. But when has this identity been 'national'? Were the Jews a people, by the same token as the French and Germans became a people?

By positing initially that the Jews are 'the conscious and deliberate heirs of the people of the Kingdom of Judah, a kingdom extinguished in the second decade of the sixth century B.C.', Toynbee gives himself the right to call the Jews a people and the identity the Jews have sought to maintain a 'national identity'. But, in a way, he contradicts his own interpretation, since he rightly acknowledges that the vast majority of Jews have, over these twenty-five centuries, regularly preferred to remain in the diaspora (*ibid.*, page 484).

The vitality of the Jewish diaspora and its significance, for mankind as a whole, as being the probable 'wave of the future', is brought out by the contrast between the steady success of the diaspora in surviving – in spite of penalizations, persecutions and massacres – and the unsatisfactoriness of all attempts up to date, since the Babylonian Captivity, to re-establish a Jewish State on Palestinian soil. The first of these attempts was made – with the permission and good will of the founder of the Achaemenian Empire, Cyrus – within less than half a century after Nebuchadnezzar had extinguished the Kingdom of Judah and had deported its notables to Babylonia. The latest attempt is being made in our day. It is noteworthy, however, that at all times when it was open to the Jews in diaspora to emigrate to a Jewish State in Palestine, a great majority of them have invariably preferred to remain in diaspora. This was so in the year 539–538 B.C., it is so today; and it has always been so all through the intervening twenty-five centuries.

If this has been so, and how can we deny it, is the identity that the Jews have sought to preserve really a national one? United across frontiers by a religion, but accepting the diaspora even when they had the opportunity of ending it, they were not perhaps a 'religious community like the rest' but nor were they a 'nation like the rest'. This peculiarity does not seem mysterious to me. On the one hand, the Jews, even if they were Gentiles converted to Judaism, had a tendency to see themselves, or to be seen by the society around them, as the descendants of the Palestinians. Religion itself helped to give its followers a more or less mythical or illusory awareness of being a people and not merely a Church.

On the other hand, the beliefs and moral prescriptions of Judaism influenced the whole of their existence, both sacred and secular, and thus determined, so to speak, a way of life. Thus the religious community became a cultural one.

The attitude of the societies in the midst of which the Jews lived made this 'cultural peculiarity' more marked. In so far as the Jews were exposed to suspicion or persecution, they reacted by stressing their originality, they made themselves autonomous, they sought to be self-sufficient, to find in the Jewish community what other men found in manifold communities, religious, political and cultural. Shut up in ghettoes, the Jewish community inevitably became a quasi-national one since the Jews had no other country. Having emerged from the ghettoes, and been authorized to participate in the social activities of their Christian milieu, the Jews preserved or lost the faith of their ancestors, and accepted or rejected assimilation (in the sense in which this would involve the loss of the specifically Jewish culture), but, at least in the Western world, the vast majority of them became citizens of the countries that had received them, without experiencing any rending conflict between their French or German citizenship and their membership of the Jewish community. Within a liberal civilization, which tolerated the Jewish along with other religions and granted the same rights to all individuals, the Jews, even those who were believers and attached to their traditions, did not feel 'dejudaized' because they were French or German citizens. The adjective 'Jewish' applied to a religion and not to a nation. The first Zionists were recruited not among the orthodox but among Jews modern in their outlook.

Is it contrary to or consistent with the inspiration of the sacred books and with the vocation of those who believe in the God of Isaac and Jacob, that Jews of the diaspora should form a nation, with a territory, a State (secular), an army and, inevitably, at the same time, friends and enemies, wars and injustices, reverses and triumphs and the historical procession of combat and cruelty? I should be angry with myself if I were to give a categorical answer, which might shock certain of my readers. But the great man to whom this book is dedicated respected above all the truth and those who pursued it sincerely.

Let us ponder the relations between Israel and the Jewish religion, that present-day form of the everlasting dialogue within Judaism between nationalism (the pact between God and His people) and the universal (the one God, the God of all mankind).

The foundation in Palestine of a State which claims that it is secular and the majority of whose inhabitants come from the Jewish communities of the diaspora, does not represent an episode in the sacred history, it cannot be interpreted as the fulfilment of eschatological promises. Despite the quotations that might be borrowed from the Bible or the Talmud, to interpret the State of Israel in terms of the millenarian promises would be to prostitute the faith, to reduce it to its pre-prophetic level. All Jews, believers and unbelievers, citizens of Israel or not, have to recognize the creation of the State of Israel as an episode in a completely human history, not as an end or a turning-point in the history of the Jewish people in its relation to its God.

As a secular event, is it the State of Israel alone that will henceforth offer the Jews a chance to live their lives fully, to realize fully their 'Judaism'? Even expressed interrogatively, such remarks, I must admit, seem to me almost devoid of meaning as well as being irritating. For believers and even for the orthodox, the best, the only way of being a good Jew is surely to obey the commandments, in the letter and the spirit.[1] There is no need at all to live in Israel in order to realize one's Judaism, if this is defined by a faith and by religious observance. If, on the other hand, we see Judaism as defined by a culture, there is no doubt that this culture will be more Jewish in Israel than in the diaspora. But for the past two thousand five hundred years, in so far as it has not become confused with religion, Jewish culture has varied with the country and the age. Israeli culture will be different from that of the yiddish-speaking Ashkenazim communities of Poland and Russia, just as Ashkenazim culture in the nineteenth century differed in its turn from that of the Sephardim Jews of the eleventh century in the Mediterranean basin. The culture that will arise in Israel will be just as much stamped by its particular circumstances as that of any

---

[1] I would no longer write this sentence today, which simplifies a complex problem.

Jewish community. It will not be, it cannot be the culture of all Jews throughout the world. Is it going to be said that it alone will be a culture in the full sense of the word because it alone will benefit from a national framework and political independence? Only the Jews of Israel will belong to the State that is closely linked with their Judaism. Will this be an advantage or an obstacle, a source of weakness or of strength? The Israelis refuse to look on their God and their State in the way in which both were looked on in the time of King David. The Israeli State is secular[1] and the more enlightened believers in Israel love a God who imposes particular obligations on the Jews but who is still the God of all mankind.

It seemed to me in Israel that the 'national ideology' which is taught to recruits coming from many countries in Europe and the Near East, was tending to establish a continuity between the Kingdoms of Israel and Judah and the State of Israel after the second world war. The Bible serves as much as a history book as a sacred text. The Israelis I met were all fervent readers of the Bible even if they did not believe in God. They wanted Israel to be a State 'just like the rest', they wanted a country for themselves, like that which other men have (especially other Europeans). I can understand this aspiration to a country which could no longer be refused us. But for the majority of Jews it will stay unsatisfied, and even the Israelis are not going to be 'citizens just like the rest' of a 'country just like the rest'.

In Israel, believers and rationalists will still be uncertain about the meaning of their joint venture. The Jews who have come from Russia, Poland and Europe have no *spontaneous* feelings of solidarity with those from the Yemen or Morocco. Even supposing that they are all descended from the Jews of Palestine – which is doubtful – the two thousand five hundred years that have elapsed since the diaspora started have wiped away the consciousness of this common origin. The original community is invoked in order to create a national community, the object of a venture pursued in the name of an archaizing ideology. The spirit of this venture is not religious but political, although they count on the strength of a religious tradition to sustain it, just as

[1] This formula is not entirely true. The relations between the State of Israel and the Church would call for a lengthy study (1967).

they count on the financial resources of those Jews who refuse to become Israelis to provide Israel with its means of subsistence. Neither the Israeli believers, closer to their 'co-religionists' of the diaspora than their fellow-countrymen, who were only looking in the Promised Land for a country in the modern and European sense of the word, nor the unbelievers, passionately attached to their brand-new State but who justify it by memories of a kingdom that vanished more than two thousand years ago, are like the French or the English, rooted in their own soil and conscious of having done great things together in the past and of wanting to do more in the future; they have no difficulty in distinguishing their national community from the Church. (Once more I am thinking above all of European non-Jews. Away from Europe, 'religious community' and 'cultural community' are often confused, though neither aspires to political fulfilment or military sovereignty.)

For genuinely religious Israelis, the State of Israel is not essential:[1] one can be a good Jew in Babylon as easily as in Jerusalem. For unbelievers in Israel, the State will finally enable Jews to have their own country but the Israeli nation has yet to be created: even supposing that the Jews of the Kingdom of Judah were a nation, they lost their nationality during the 2,500 years of the diaspora, and must win it back out of the Promised Land. Neither believers nor unbelievers will be able truly to separate themselves from the diaspora, neither will be able to put an end to the tragic destiny or, if you prefer, to the paradoxical and hence threatened existence of Judaism, an existence the more threatened the more paradoxical it is, and the more paradoxical the more contradictory the impression it gives of itself to observers in the world outside. If the Jews, like the faithful of all salvationist religions, adore the same God but belong to different nations, they have a chance of sharing the common fate, although, if they are not amenable to the teachings of the two religions springing from the Old Testament, they risk being the object of the hatred or contempt of fanatics for as long as they live among Christians or Muslims. On the other hand, to the extent that, either in reaction against their milieu or else spontaneously, they declare themselves to be the 'people of David'

[1] This formula too now appears to me over-simplified (1967).

or a 'Jewish nation', they place themselves outside the common lot in this age of nationalities. It was the illusion of the Zionists that they would overcome this paradox: since the Jews were not fully accepted by nations, they would form their own nation. They produced the opposite result: since not all Jews can or will go back to Palestine, their community, which is neither purely a religious one nor a fully national one, seems more paradoxical still. The secular State of Israel, built and preserved by the sword, is also paradoxical both in itself and in relation to the diaspora.

* * *

In the foregoing pages, I have attempted to analyse without passing judgment, to write neither as a believer nor as an unbeliever. It goes without saying, however, that this seeming impartiality, even if I have not violated it, will pass for a form of commitment[1] with my 'co-religionists' who are committed in another direction (Israelis or orthodox Jews). Let us drop the impersonal style and go over to the first person.

I am a citizen of France and not of Israel. I am not a believer, at least in the common sense of that word. As Spinoza said, I cannot believe that God has ever concluded a pact with any people as such. A people draws nearer to God in so far as it overcomes its tribal pride and conforms to the commandments of the law or of love. Everyone has the right to his own country, and it is natural to be attached to a group. But the group that believes it has a divine mission is the one most lacking in the religious spirit (as I conceive of it, naturally). Judaism includes both nationalism and universalism, and it is the second which seems to me to answer to the genuine vocation of Judaism and of all religions of salvation. The building of a State in Palestine which proclaims itself to be continuing the Kingdom of Judah, seems to me a historical accident to which only the idolator, who accords a supreme value to the nation, will lend a truly religious meaning.

For all Jews, the State of Israel represents a great event in secular history. It cannot but arouse strong feelings in all of us.

[1] Or worse still, a form of hostility (1967).

A Jew, even if he has lost his faith, cannot be indifferent to Israel's fate. Personally, I have been deeply affected by what Arthur Koestler (not without having analysed it rationally) called a 'miracle', and what I would call the epic story of the pioneers of Israel. Whatever happens in the future, the Israelis won their independence in the 'war of liberation', and they are protecting it jealously thanks to the strength of their army, which is constantly on the alert; they have achieved great military renown. They have offered hundred of thousands of Jews a refuge. They have changed the image that non-Jews had of Jews. They have proved that Jews could once again, as in the days of the Roman Empire, win a reputation for martial valour. From many points of view, what the Jews have done in Israel does credit to Judaism and to the human race as a whole.

But Israel would not belong to secular history if she were not stamped with the imperfections of all human creations. Or rather, as the expression of a paradoxical history, she remains oddly paradoxical herself. The land for the State of Israel was bought in the first place from its Muslim owners with money collected by the Jews of the diaspora; the flight of the Muslims at the start of the 'war of liberation' enabled them to take possession of a territory containing the Holy Places of the three religions of salvation. The Israelis assert, rightly, that they did not chase the Muslims out, but that they left hoping to return victorious. But these vicissitudes matter less in Arab eyes than one brutal fact: the Muslims, who had been settled in Palestine for more than ten centuries, had to make way for Jews claiming to be reviving the tradition of the Kingdom of Judah.

That the Israelis should have invoked historical rights of priority convinces nobody. After a few centuries a prescription operates. When Nehru took over Goa by force, denying claims based on five centuries of occupation, Western opinion was indignant (or, at least, displayed indignation, whether sincere or feigned). How could it recognize a claim to ownership dating back more than two thousand years? The State of Israel has been carved out by the sword – in this respect the Jews have managed to take faithfully after the Gentiles. But, by the same token, the hostility of the Arab world becomes understandable, inevitable and, in all probability, irreducible.

For the time being, one million seven hundred thousand Jews[1] (rather less than half of them from Europe) can manage to put into the field an army superior on its own to the coalition of all the armies of the Arab States in the Near East. The local balance of strength is in Israel's favour; the rivalry of the Great Powers helps to maintain this balance. The United States grants a certain protection to the Israeli State while the Soviet Union wants to display its hostility to it rather than destroy it. One of the Powers wants a reconciliation, the other wants to prevent it. The latter obviously is winning the day: even if it is relatively easy to stop small States from fighting each other to the death, how can they be forced to agree?

The foreseeable future of Israel, over the coming years and perhaps for much longer, will still be that of a threatened people, living in a sort of fortified camp and relying on its armies for survival. Having been born by the sword, Israel can but, at the present moment, live by the sword, beneath the threat of another sword (less keen than its own for the time being). Admittedly, it is easy to understand that those who have survived the greatest massacres in history should have vowed never again to face the assassin's knife with bare hands. But nor can we conceal from ourselves the fact that the Israelis have chosen to live dangerously, at the point where twin lines of strategy converge and in a part of the world that has been haunted by the gods and trampled on by soldiers? They have become a pawn on the international chessboard, condemned to take part in the diabolical game of 'power politics', and they are citizens of a State that has baptized its selfishness as sacred. But, sacred or not, this is the selfishness of a State that will never number more than a few million citizens, on a territory that is lilliputian by the standards of modern methods of transport and destruction.

I do not want to exclude the hypothesis of a reconciliation between Israel and her neighbours, though I hold it to be lastingly improbable. The Christian kingdom of Jerusalem lasted two centuries, not two decades or two generations; for all that, it was never accepted by the Muslims. In a cold war with its neighbours, the State of Israel is doomed to a heroic but limited destiny. It will only live if it turns Jews from Morocco, Tunisia and

[1] Two and a half millions now (1967).

the Yemen into citizens of a modern State. Lacking a sufficiently large population, Israel will be debarred from certain scientific and technological undertakings that demand big concentrations of material means; she will need to struggle constantly against the temptations of facility to continue to participate honourably in our culture. Despite her geography, Israel will have to remain an integral part of Western civilization, at least until such time as the Muslim world has effected its own conversion to modernity.

In spite of the size of the task which the Jews from Europe and the United States have set themselves in Palestine – the integration of several hundred thousand, or, if need be, two or three million non-Western Jews into a Western-type nation – the Israeli enterprise is a provincial one in the world of the twentieth century.[1] In a way, Israel will have all the more chance of not declining into a levantine State the less she turns in on herself, the more she remains in touch with Europe and the United States. We must hope that the selfishness necessary to a militant nationalism does not contradict the need to keep frontiers open.

If Judaism were to become identified with a small State in the Near East, it would no longer be part of the world's history. I can understand that a number of Jews, wearied by misfortune and persecution, should dream of such a way out. But it is only a dream; that way out is closed to us because Israel and the Jewish communities of the diaspora will exist side by side, like the Jews of Babylon and those of Palestine in the last centuries before Christ. A total assimilation and a change of name can offer this hoped-for way out to Jews seen as individuals. But it has not yet been given to the Jews as a whole to overcome the paradox inherited from more than twenty centuries of history. Having lived among Muslims and Christians, that is the faithful of the religions which emerged from Judaism, the Jews have been and are, in their own eyes as well as the eyes of those around them, the heirs of the people of David, a people chosen by God but which did not recognize Christ the Saviour, a people which believes in the God of all mankind but also believes itself to

---

[1] I would no longer write this today (1967).

be bound to him by a peculiar bond. Believer, orthodox or liberal, it hardly matters, nothing would ever make me accept that a State, even one rooted in the Promised Land, can claim to embody a faith that is miserably diminished if it is not offered to all men. As an unbeliever (at least in relation to the normal interpretation of that term), I shall not begrudge Israel my sympathy, but I do refuse her a national loyalty which goes to my own country. Even though 'assimilated' and lost to a truly Jewish culture, I have not betrayed what is best in the religious message of Judaism if, beyond my national attachments, I have preserved the sense of universal values in knowledge and in action.

What the Jews have to say to humanity will never be translated into the language of arms.

The foregoing article brought me a considerable postbag. The *Figaro Littéraire* published extracts from these letters. I replied in the issue of March 17, 1962 with the following postscript.

Postscript

I had expressed the hope that my article on *The Jews and the State of Israel* would not give offence to any of my 'co-religionists'. This hope was not, and probably could not have been, fulfilled. I was wrong to have forgotten that it may be best not to discuss certain problems. As survivors of the greatest massacre in their own history and in modern history, the Jews today have every right to be touchy. And the Israelis, a nation under arms and surrounded by enemies, have the right to be annoyed by the remarks of a Jew who declares himself sympathetic but refuses to commit himself.

It goes without saying, from the outset, that I have never claimed to speak on behalf of anybody but myself. How could it be otherwise? In the present-day world, a Jew has to choose himself, by assuming his Judaism in one way or another. A Frenchman who is a Christian but who has lost his faith does not have to assume his Christianity; he is still a Frenchman just like the rest. Religion is a private matter and the State does not distinguish between believers and unbelievers. A Jew who has lost his faith and no longer goes regularly to the synagogue remains a Jew, but he questions himself about the meaning of that word.

At times the Jew in France or England who no longer takes part in a truly Jewish culture gets his Judaism from the world around him and from anti-semitism. It is to this, so to speak, 'de-judaized' Jew that Jean-Paul Sartre's *Reflections on the Jewish Question* apply. But however assimilated he is or reckons he is, the Jew keeps a feeling of solidarity both with his ancestors and with the other Jewish communities of the diaspora. Especially in our own day, after Hitler's persecutions, a Jew cannot flee from his destiny and ignore those who, in other places, have believed or do believe in the same God of Isaac and of Jacob, the God of his ancestors.

Once this solidarity has been admitted and, as it were, lived, several courses are open to each one of us. I do not doubt for a moment that an Israeli nation has been born in Palestine. I can understand that Jews should choose Israeli nationality: I shall neither blame nor extol those who do so choose. But this does not mean that a different choice is to be condemned. The decision belongs to each individual. It is true, as a correspondent has written to me, that there exist individual cases of double nationality. I do not believe that a group, such as the Jewish group, can aspire to the privilege of double nationality. That goes without saying, my readers will answer. I agree, but if it goes without saying, is it so serious to say it?

When I brought up the hypothesis of a possible divergence between the national interests of France and those of Israel, I was not the prisoner of the age-old anguish of the persecuted, nor was I being subtly machiavellian. As I see it, the end of the Algerian war does not signify the end of the friendship between France and Israel. How many Israelis, over the past few years, have not expressed to me their sorrow that the friendship which they hoped would be an enduring one between France and Israel seemed founded on a common hostility! Several of the members of the Franco-Israeli Society supported a liberal solution in Algeria, although they knew that a number of Jews would leave an independent Algeria.

Some of my readers are amazed that I can recommend assimilation after the horrors of the recent past. But I have not recommended assimilation at all: a Jew who wants to be a French citizen can keep jealously intact the culture and the religion that he has received as his inheritance. What we must know is whether he wants to belong fully to the nation which is, by birth and by desire, his own. To this question my answer is yes. I am inhibited neither by the events of yesterday which some people quote at me, nor the eventualities of the future evoked by others, nor the persistence of anti-semitism. We Jews will live dangerously, in Israel or elsewhere, whether we like it or not. The age of contempt may return. But the Israelis, who have shown such great courage, would be contradicting themselves if they criticized the Jews of the diaspora, on the pretext that the latter risk, some day, being deprived of the nationality which they want to be complete and unqualified.

But how are the moral links between the Jews in Israel and those of the diaspora to be preserved? I am not unaware of the seriousness of the question I have been asked, although I do not have, obviously, any miraculous, ready-made solution by means of which Jews who are living distinct national histories can nevertheless safeguard a feeling of unity. But why should we not have faith in the future? As my friend Manès Sperber has reminded me, the Jewish communities of the diaspora have, over the centuries, managed not to lose the sense of their unique mission. The history of Judaism will be written by the Israelis and the Jews of the diaspora together. The first condition of this shared history is that they should understand and respect each other mutually. Their friendship would be shattered by a fanaticism hostile to the Jews who want to be citizens of France or the United States.

I know that those who have built and who maintain the State of Israel are quite without such fanaticism.

Index